# THE PROMISE OF ACCELERATION

# THE PROMISE OF ACCELERATION

*A Strength-Based Plan to Propel Academically Vulnerable Learners*

## SUZY PEPPER ROLLINS

Fast Lane Learning, LLC
Jacksonville Beach, Florida

**Fast Lane Learning, LLC**
**3948 3ᴿᴰ Street South #443**
**Jacksonville Beach, Florida 32250**
**www.SuzyPepperRollins.com**

Publisher's Note: This work is intended as a general information resource for teachers, school administrators, and curriculum and instruction professionals. Although the author has significant expertise in the area, neither the author nor the publisher can guarantee that any strategy, technique, or approach will work with every student.

All links in this book were active on publication date. However, links may have become inactive or modified since that date.

**The Promise of Acceleration.** -- 1st ed.

ISBN 979-8-218-15865-1

Library of Congress Control Number: 2023903789

# TABLE OF CONTENTS

# INTRODUCTION

EVERY CHILD WANTS to be successful. Even those who have gotten behind. It may not look that way, with their heads propped up on their elbows in feigned disinterest. "This is boring," they profess. Or "I could do it if I wanted." It cannot be easy for them to cross the school threshold again and again with the same results—to return to the place where failure looms.

What comes to mind when thinking about traditional remedial offerings? Probably what the research suggests. Students who have gotten into academic holes are typically provided with passive, bland work that moves backwards in an effort to plug the gaps and "catch them up." It is often out of context and typically not applied to today's learning targets. And it's hard to learn things out of context. They are more likely to have seat work, worksheets, and screens than other students who are "on track."

They are also likely to be grouped, pulled out, and even scheduled together. As other students engage in dynamic lessons, their instructional world becomes less engaging, even isolating. Less positive relationships with teachers, reduced models of success, less fun at school, always behind. As they move backwards in learning, other students move forward. Despite the best of intentions, the gaps may widen. Concerned educators wonder why they are not more motivated. Don't they even care?

Acceleration is a tactical process that reignites the motivation to learn. The mission of acceleration is to achieve success today on new learning targets. Why? Because the last thing these students need are more gaps. The bulk of acceleration instruction consists of imbedding prior knowledge just in time to latch on to something new. Acceleration students get a head start on photosynthesis or slope or "The Rime of the Ancient Mariner." What about all those gaps? They are remediated in context just in time for new learning. In other words, missing pieces are critically distributed throughout the units—place value here, decimals here, and commas there.

Remediation is often a parallel world of working on gaps that have little intersection with today's learning. Acceleration, conversely, is tightly connected to current core learning targets. It is not a separate program. The lines of remediation and acceleration merge into one mission: success today.

Acceleration can change the trajectory of academic success in students. And while acceleration is an instructional plan, it is also a mindset shift. It is a fresh start for learners who may not have experienced success in a while. In acceleration, learners are not defined by those missing pieces. It is a strategically designed plan to get students moving upward, by getting them ready for class today. Acceleration is a forward-moving, hopeful path. Because coming to school always feeling behind can bring a sense of futility and defeatism.

## HOW TO USE THIS PROFESSIONAL DEVELOPMENT WORKBOOK

The purpose of this workbook is to support individual, building or district work on acceleration. It is a professional development tool with imbedded tasks along the way. The tasks can be completed as a group or individually. The workbook begins with children—what it feels like to be behind. Next, there is a chapter with big picture ideas—The Promise of Acceleration. The remainder of the workbook has a focus on real-world implementation. From instructional strategies to communication devices to scheduling to motivating academically vulnerable learners—a plan will evolve throughout your work.

There is purposeful redundancy throughout the workbook. The reasoning behind this is that some chapters might be pulled out for large group faculty discussions. Therefore, overarching themes get reintroduced as critical background knowledge.

As you progress through your work, a clear vision with steps will develop. But acceleration is an imperfect process. The best laid plans may need adjustments to maximize success. Typically, the first change realized in acceleration learners is increased participation. After all, acceleration is about setting up success for class today as we pick up critical pieces in context. As engagement increases, academic improvement should follow.

The word "acceleration" has different meanings. When driving a vehicle, acceleration means to gain speed quickly. In physics, acceleration describes a change in velocity. Both definitions aptly describe the instructional approach detailed in subsequent pages. Rather than slow these kids down with tedium and review sheets, they are going to be accelerated just ahead of their peers. They are going to know a little about tides or chemical reactions or equivalent fractions...just in time for new learning. For the first time in possibly a while, some of their hands should pop into the air. "I Know! I Know!"

Share your success either on Twitter @myedexpert or reach out via my website: www.SuzyPepperRollins.com.

# 1

## IN THEIR SHOES: ACADEMICALLY VULNERABLE LEARNERS

WHAT CLASS MADE you cry? Was there a subject or a particular course in which you felt unprepared or even overwhelmed? Revisit that experience. Consider how you felt sitting in that desk. What strategies did you implement to improve your situation? How was your motivation impacted? Did you continue to pursue that subject at higher levels after the experience?

Now, consider what it might be like to experience academic vulnerability for a prolonged period. A grading cycle, a year...multiple years? What toll might that take on your academic and emotional readiness to learn? Respond below:

### YOUR TURN:

The class/course that was most difficult for me was:

The reason(s) it was difficult:

I responded to the situation by: (Ideas: avoidance, seeking help from others, withdrawal, rising to the challenge...)

If I had remained in this academically vulnerable position for a long time...

Educators typically have a history of academic success, including on-time grade promotion, high school graduation, college admission, and even graduate school. Therefore, it might be difficult for those with mental portfolios of positive educational experiences to understand the mindset of many of our academically vulnerable learners. Why don't these students just work harder? How is it possible that they arrive without materials...and sometimes not even on time? Don't they care?

The behaviors of some of these learners might signal a nonchalant, even callous, lack of concern about the importance of their education. Some will do just about anything to avoid schoolwork at all. They show up late and look for opportunities to roam the hallways. They are present simply because it is required by law...or their parents. Others exhibit an edgy temperament, perhaps as a shield to cover embarrassment over their academic situation. And there are those who, despite their academic hardships, continue to work hard every day, determined to improve.

To describe these learners as vulnerable may seem a stretch. After all, they may have experienced suspensions, grade-level retentions, absenteeism, or been enrolled in a string of academic interventions. They might be sitting in class with their arms folded defensively or heads pancaked on the desk. And sometimes, their own decisions have impacted their current situation. But vulnerable they are, perhaps even fragile. Of course, there are degrees of academic vulnerability. Some learners have just begun to slip behind; others have been in academic holes for a while. Some students are right at the cusp of passing high stakes tests; others are significantly below the cut score. There are students who are behind in credits for graduation and/or failing multiple courses. For many, academic vulnerability may look like difficulty in reading or math. Each of these students has a different back story about how they got to this place in which academic interventions are employed.

## PARTICULARLY VULNERABLE LEARNERS

Throughout the K-12 academic journey, there are innumerable opportunities to fall behind, misunderstand a concept, or not commit something to long term memory. Every learner can slip into academic vulnerability at some juncture. But there are particularly tender points along their school journeys. For example, researchers Morgan, Farkas, and Wu (2012) found that fifth graders who were weak readers were more likely to describe themselves as sad, lonely, unpopular, and even angry. Other researchers have noted that students who are not faring well in reading are more likely to legitimately be ill with nausea and headaches. As they get older, these readers are more likely to develop anxiety, depression, and even misconduct (Galuschka & Schulte-Korne, 2016). Even with our youngest learners, weak reading in first grade can be a predictor of behavioral issues in third. And reading issues that continue into adulthood can even be a predictor for unemployment, underemployment, and poverty (Adult Literacy Facts, 2019). In sum, reading across grade levels and content is an area of vulnerability.

Students who have experienced one or more grade level retentions are a group with high vulnerability as well. Researchers have studied retention for decades with the same guidance for educators: the practice does not improve academic success. In research analyzing seventeen studies on the subject, grade level retention was deemed a predictor of dropout (Jimerson, Anderson, and Whipple, 2002). Retention, as counterintuitive as it may seem, has proven to be less positive than promotion to the next grade.

What about retention in lower grades? Research shows that in lower grades, students might exhibit short term gains, only to plummet later and, again, be more likely candidates to dropout (Silberglitt, Jimerson, Burns, & Appleton, 2006). In sum, children retained in lower grades tend to decline below their socially promoted peers who were equally under-performing. Researchers found that retained students are not just more likely to dropout, but also more likely to exhibit behavioral issues, including aggressiveness and lack of motivation (Anderson, Whipple, & Jimerson, 2003). Furthermore, some studies consider retention to be a trauma-inducing experience for children. Shame, embarrassment, and a loss of friends can accompany retention.

What about students whose class participation has diminished? Informal observations often reveal that by middle and high school, fewer hands are in the air to respond to questions. As students get older, their self-efficacy—their own perception of their capabilities on a task—tends to decline. Unlike lower grades, these learners have an academic history. Some have developed an inner voice telling them they are incapable of the work and are consequently less open to engagement...and risk of failure.

A learner's self-efficacy is especially important for new learning. It is one of the elements that signals to students to jump in on a task—that they have a shot at success. Students who deem themselves incapable of experiencing success on tasks tend to understandably refrain from participating. Or, if they attempt the task and hit an obstacle, they withdraw quickly, afraid to fail again (Brophy, 2010). As they get older, they might fear embarrassment in front of their peers, and self-protect. "This task is stupid." "I could do it if I wanted...Can I go to the nurse?"

Research reveals that around seventh grade, academic self-efficacy declines significantly (Schunk & Meece, 2006). Districts report that the eighth and ninth grade years prove particularly challenging for students. In gathering their resources to support learners, many school leaders examine eighth grade reading scores, as well as attendance and suspension rates.

A case can be made that these vulnerable learners, particularly as they get older, are experiencing more stress than higher performing students. Their history of academic struggles often instills a perception that participating in new learning is risky. The real possibility of further failure looms in their minds. Learners who are experiencing considerable levels of stress and even anxiety have more difficulty learning. As the brain transitions to survival mode, learning something new might become secondary. Higher level thinking can get sacrificed, as the ability to process and store information diminishes. Conversely, learners who are more relaxed are better at solving problems, exhibit higher levels of focus, and behave more positively (Willis, 2006).

Low grades, reading issues, declining academic self-confidence, reluctance to participate in class, low scores on high stakes tests. These are potential indicators of academic vulnerability. An additional special group of learners who might not be on the radar for support are learners who have difficulty sustaining attention. More likely to be male, their brains have increased difficulty in following instructions, keeping organized, attending to tedious, unrelatable tasks, and sometimes just sitting for a long period of time. Their impulsivity can hinder learning as well as their often-weaker memories. They need movement, exciting tasks, novelty, and organizational support. Juxtapose their learning traits with the typical day in school of rapid-fire, often sit still delivery. As a group, these learners experience academic underperformance. Imposing additional passive remedial experiences to "catch them up" can be a problematic misfit. Sadly, they can also misinterpret the large amount of redirection from teachers throughout the day as not even being liked by educators. (Rollins, 2020).

English learners, as a group, are underperforming in math and reading. In fourth grade reading and eighth grade math, for example, there is a 40% gap between ELL and other students (Murphey, 2014). Just one-third of English learners scored basic or above on the math portion of the National Assessment of Educational Progress (NAEP) test, compared to 75% of other learners in our buildings. This trend, unfortunately, continues beyond K-12. One study indicates that just 19% will advance to four-year colleges, compared to 43% of monolingual students (Kanno & Cromley, 2015). And of English learners who enter college, just 12% complete four-year programs within eight years. The challenges in learning content in chemistry, biology, or history in a new language are daunting.

There are students who slip in and out of academic vulnerability. They dip and recover. Others experience more chronic academic underachievement. One can make the case that it takes courage for those who have experienced failure for a long time to simply come to school. Test scores are but one indicator of academic vulnerability. But vulnerability can also be observed through diminished academic confidence, a reluctance to participate in class, attendance, and/or behavioral changes.

Reflect upon academic vulnerability. Are their students who might benefit from a different approach to increasing academic success? Organize your thoughts on the next "Your Turn."

---

### YOUR TURN:

Reflect and collaborate on academic vulnerability in your building(s). Which learners might benefit from additional support? Consider: reading, math, classroom engagement, language issues, recent drops in grades, course failure, attendance, and/or behavioral changes.

---

## RESPONDING TO THE NEEDS OF VULNERABLE LEARNERS

The path from academic vulnerability to success may require a departure from current practices. To accelerate learning—to get them on pace with peers and perhaps even beyond—vulnerable students need the most impactful practices available. Academic motivation—jumping in to learn something new—relies on providing captivating, relevant tasks that are within learners' grasps. Learners with low self-efficacy benefit from collaborating with highly self-confident teachers who utilize student-centered instruction. This enables students to regain a measure of autonomy over their own learning. Real accomplishments, student autonomy, and genuine success—even small bursts in the beginning—can reignite motivation.

What often occurs, however, with academically vulnerable learners is quite different. In a well-intentioned effort to close deficits, struggling learners are often grouped together, which reduces their interactions with peer models of success. This practice can reduce opportunities for vicarious success, a motivator in learning. Interactions with more successful, engaged peers can boost learning. Courseware or remedial worksheets are often a mainstay for struggling learners, which limit collaborative opportunities with teachers or peers. An overreliance on prescribed courseware can reduce feedback from educators. Ongoing growth-oriented feedback is essential to new learning; in fact, it is one of the most effective tools for moving students upward. Rather than opportunities for engaging, innovative work, they are often relegated to passive, isolating work. Grouping students with deficits together and increasing passive tasks while reducing collaboration in an effort to "catch them up" is a problematic instructional formula. In addition, a considerable amount of that work may involve going back...and back...and back.

One study explains a downward spiral with middle schoolers that occurs when they are provided few opportunities for academic decision making combined with less time with teachers (Eccles and colleagues, 1993). Another large 6-12 study reveals that the highest levels of engagement during the school day occurs when working in labs and during group work. The lowest level of engagement? When teachers are talking. (Yair, 2000).

In the reading arena, this phenomenon of how skills gaps can actually widen between vulnerable and more successful learners is sometimes referred to as the "Matthew Effect" (Stanovich, 1986). Stronger readers tend to enjoy reading, so they read more often. It gives them pleasure and they receive positive feedback. Their skills improve and they become increasingly proficient. Weaker readers often avoid reading. Therefore, the gap in reading may widen, despite our best efforts. One can make the case for a similar pattern in math. Learners who have lost confidence in their math capabilities may withdraw from tasks entirely or surrender quickly when the work gets challenging. As they shut down, other, more confident learners move upward. More deficits may develop.

Prescribed courseware can certainly be strategically incorporated as part of a support plan for academically vulnerable students. But some preassessments in these programs send the students with the weakest skills the farthest back. How will they ever catch up? How will the work they are doing support new learning today... or are the tasks entirely remedial? The academic plan developed for learners who have gotten behind should be tactically developed with vulnerable children in mind.

---

## YOUR TURN:

Create a visual image of academic vulnerability. This might look like: a cycle, a cause and effect, compare/contrast, or a K-12 timeline.

---

## PAST LEARNING CHALLENGES IMPACT NEW LEARNING

Vulnerable learners arrive to class with their academic baggage in tow. Gaps in learning, previous low grades, low self-confidence, and a learned reluctance to openly participate influence efforts today. Often, learning something new depends on an understanding of a past target. It can be difficult for them to truly get a fresh start.

An issue often mentioned regarding academically vulnerable learners is their motivation—or lack thereof. As evidence of their academic deficits mount, their motivation (understandably) tends to decline. (Chapter 5 is all about motivation!) This may seem counterintuitive to teachers, leaders, and parents. Just work harder, the adults insist. But learning is risky. All day long, educators implore learners to try something new: a physics lab, a poem by Shakespeare, or a math problem on slope. Successful students with a positive history of academic risk-taking often jump right in—no warning lights flash. But for students with failure histories, caution is their shield. Three underpinnings to enhance motivation for all students, but particularly for this group are: self-efficacy, value of the task, and learning environment (Rollins, 2020).

As teachers are introducing a task, learners' brains are quickly weighing the level of risk involved. Is the potential reward of expending effort on the task worth the risk of failure? A task that is tedious and seems to lack value will yield little motivation from this group of learners. Captivating, intriguing tasks are more worth the risk.

But value is not enough—the task must fall within their own perception of their capabilities. Tasks that are too easy can reduce motivation, tasks that are beyond their range are also problematic. Students' personal perceptions of their skills—and these may not be entirely accurate—contribute to their willingness to work on a task. Younger students are often more self-efficacious and willing to raise their hands to volunteer information or embark on a new task. Older ones, however, may have developed a sense that the answer in their heads is probably not right anyway, so they don't want to take a chance on embarrassment. Their hands remain down.

In addition, consider the prerequisite skills gaps accumulated along the way, such as fractions, decimals, place value, integer rules, percentages, commas, parts of speech...a formidable list. Vulnerable learners might be initially intrigued by a new concept but reduce engagement when they realize that fractions (or other missing skills) are once again required for success. "I didn't do well in fractions before." As they get older, these skills deficits can result in more errors and a sea of red on returned papers. If they exert effort on the work and do not realize any success or progress, this can contribute to further disengagement. Through their lens, the work expended did not provide a successful return.

Failure hurts. The brain responds to the hurt by protecting the child. They may become increasingly hesitant to answer questions. They might conceal their work or copy from a neighbor. Their more successful classmates embark on the task—fueled by success and positive feedback—and fill the void of classroom participation.

Students with a history of failure learn to view graded assessments differently as well. Struggling learners perceive low scores on tests as further proof of their failure, not as opportunities for growth. These grades can lead to a further decline in motivation (Davies, 2007). Students with a history of academic success, however, tend to enjoy getting grades and perceive the grading system as fair. They are better at test-taking and demonstrate higher levels of perseverance during testing (Harlen & Crick, 2003). Successful learners may be the ones asking, "Can we take a grade on this?"

This evidence plays out when tests are returned in class. Successful learners might share their scores with their neighbors and neatly arrange them in their binders. Vulnerable learners often rip them, wad them, toss them...just get rid of the evidence. Of course, grades are a necessary part of school. But, by understanding the mindset of vulnerable learners, a more positive path is a steady stream of soft, ungraded formative assessments to prepare for the graded assessments.

Students who have struggled require greater assurances from educators, but it must be genuine, particularly for older students. They know they are behind. A welcome when they arrive and a pencil when they need one certainly make a difference. But they also need concrete signs of improvement—something to put on the refrigerator. Acceleration can be that academic pivot. Acceleration can be a genuine fresh start.

## VISION

Today, spreadsheets packed with data drive instruction. A click of a button provides color-coded cells of deficits, deficits, deficits. It may be difficult to look at those spreadsheets and not go back, back, back. Yes, deficits need to be addressed. But today's learning targets, for which they might be unprepared, are the instructional priority. A student who is behind in reading might have difficulty with today's lesson on "Beowulf" or *The Great Gatsby*. Finding the area of a triangle requires an understanding of base and height. How do we lift students with gaps up to master new learning? How can we create learning experiences that both address the past, but with a hopeful eye on the future?

That is the promise of acceleration, a process that revisits past deficits, but tactically in the context of new learning...and just in time. Acceleration, though not perfect, offers a forward-moving plan that prepares students for success on new concepts today, so that may learn alongside their peers, right where they belong.

Clarify the vision for academically vulnerable learners in the following "Your Turn." What outcomes will be realized? What works for academically vulnerable learners?

---

### YOUR TURN:

What outcomes do you want to see for academically vulnerable learners? What are your hopes for them?

Describe, in words or a graphic, the best instructional approach for learners who have gotten behind? What works best for these learners?

---

## SUMMARY

The purpose of this first chapter is to reflect upon—to take a new look at—academically vulnerable learners. What must it feel like to arrive at the same place every day and meet the same academic fate? Often times, they are relegated to prescribed remedial courseware, which brings fewer opportunities to engage with teachers or other students. Or they are grouped together with others who are equally behind and similarly non-participatory.

Acceleration offers a different path forward—a chance to get those hands back up in the air. Because one thing every educator knows for certain: It is difficult to teach a child who has lost hope.

# 2

## THE PROMISE OF ACCELERATION

The purpose of chapter one was to step into the sneakers of academically vulnerable learners. And while their paths vary, one common feature is they bring their academic histories to school with them every day. Their missing academic pieces plus their drop in confidence can make learning something new more challenging. Secondly, chapter one talked about the instructional response that is often employed for these learners. Largely deficit based, they spend a significant portion of their days in backward movement, often grouped with other learners who are also not experiencing much success. This chapter is about a different mission—a strength-based, hopeful path—that spends time on deficits, but also moves them forward. But those nagging deficits—let's begin there...

The K-12 academic journey is a long one. Learners spend over two thousand days of their lives in class. Each day—each hour—is an opportunity to miss something, not catch on, or simply forget what was learned. We all have gaps. For example, the following are things likely learned in school. Take the quiz. What do you remember? What have you forgotten? Why?

---

### YOUR TURN:

What do You Remember from School?

1. What is the formula for the surface area of a cylinder?

2. "All that glitters is not gold." This quote is from which work by Shakespeare?

3. What is the function of the vacuole in plant and animal cells?

4. What is 3/5 as a decimal?

5. Name one year in which Henry VIII reigned.

6. What classification lies between phylum and domain?

7. What is the difference between acceleration and velocity?

8. "Donald's dog dragged the donuts." What literacy device is used?

---

How did you fare on the quiz? Now, take a second look at the questions on the quiz above. Which of these might pose a barrier to new learning? Are there math skills or formulas that will be relied upon for impending learning targets? Does an upcoming science unit build on an understanding of cells gleaned from prior years? Will a new ELA unit rely on knowledge of literary devices? A "yes" answer moves those prerequisite skills to a priority. Are there items on the quiz that might *not* be needed for what is about to be taught? The year Henry VIII reigned? The quote from Shakespeare?

Only the missing pieces critical to mastering upcoming new learning targets make the list for acceleration, as opposed to the more extensive—and often out-of-context—laundry list in wholescale remediation. In the acceleration process, all gaps are not equal. Because acceleration is about providing what the brain needs right now to learn something new. And that's exciting!

Acceleration is a process designed to move students forward and upward. Rather than a laundry list of deficits, acceleration utilizes just-in-time remediation. Instead of tackling everything a child missed, the plan is to prepare them for new learning—to provide what they need to perform well in class right now, today.

Critical unfinished learning pieces are distributed throughout the learning targets right when they are needed for new learning. Concrete devices are provided to support learning, such as bookmarks with formulas or a cheat sheet on figurative language. These devices—either paper or digital—provide support at learners' fingertips. So, if negative numbers are upcoming in math today, teachers equip acceleration students with handy sticky notes of integer rules in their binders. This prepares them for new learning. The conversation in acceleration is "It's been a while since you've seen place value, so here's a visual for you on this anchor chart." Just-in-time remediation enables students to apply the weak/forgotten skill in context right when they need it. Learning is easier and more productive when it is in context, applied, and growth is realized.

Consider the difference between acceleration and remediation on just this point of missing skills. In traditional remediation, learners might be reviewing skills they are not even using today. They might not be doing any better in class today than they were yesterday. Wholescale remediation is a parallel instructional world that may not intersect with—or directly impact—new classroom learning. Acceleration tactically selects one or two prerequisite skills that are urgently needed to enhance success today, not yesterday, last month, or two years ago. This approach breaks this deficit list into small, urgent, doable pieces. Rather than embarking on everything a student never got, it is quite focused on what they need today to gain academic traction. Because it is distributed just when needed, the time component is more manageable, and folded into new learning. Traditional remediation can become a world of deficits, frustration, and even futility.

The just-in-time remediation component within acceleration is a small, albeit important, part of the process. However, the big piece—around 80%—of acceleration is something quite different. Acceleration is a forward moving path that offers a fresh start for academically vulnerable learners. Acceleration can reignite engagement, renew a sense of accomplishment, and develop academic strengths. How? By equipping students with what they need to learn—by setting them up for success on today's upcoming lesson. And by crafting instructional models and experiences that spark intrinsic motivation.

---

YOUR TURN:

Consider the academic interventions in your building/district. How would you describe the overarching mission? Are some of the same students in need of interventions year after year? If so, why?

---

## ACCELERATION: THE MISSION

As discussed earlier, remediation programs often have students take a preassessment and then try to fill gaps with little connection to what students are working on today. This approach has a premise that "If we could just fill all those holes, they'd do just fine in school." The mission of acceleration is very different. The goal of acceleration is for academically vulnerable students to learn new concepts on pace with their classmates. In other words, the mission is to generate authentic success in the classroom. Today. Right now. On today's learning targets.

How are they doing? Let's look at their work—their evidence of learning—and see. Did they participate, engage with teammates, raise their hands? Because one thing we know about success: when students experience it, they tend to want more of that feeling. The mission of acceleration is ambitious, and perhaps a shift in mindset. Good day today, better day tomorrow—this plan is about rebuilding children who way back when enjoyed learning new things in school.

What can be done to change the academic trajectory of frustrated learners? How can intrinsic motivation be reignited in learners who have gotten off track? If remediation is just a small percent of acceleration, what are these students doing the other 80% of the time?

Acceleration prepares students for new learning by tactically jumping them ahead of the class. The instructional priority and bulk of time is spent on preparing them for new learning; in effect, setting them up for success. For example, if students are about to read "The Gettysburg

Address" in their core class, the acceleration group might first watch a video of an actor reenacting the speech. They might spend a few minutes looking at pictures of the cemetery or photographs of the battle. And they might pre-annotate their text with synonyms of unfamiliar words. The acceleration learners will walk into class equipped with just enough background knowledge for success. Now, when the core teacher asks if anyone knows anything about Gettysburg, they will likely pronounce that the word "score" means twenty. * More importantly, they will share their newfound prior knowledge about the incredible loss of life during the battle.

Adding decimals today? Acceleration students have already engaged in perusing local restaurant menus and adding up their pretend bills. They also have a concise decimal scaffolding device for reference, just in time for the core math class. About to kick off angles in the core class? Acceleration students have traced angles in the hallways and created sorts of acute, obtuse, and right angles. Or perhaps they constructed angles with pipe cleaners. In all of these scenarios, movement is forward, with a small amount of just-in-time remediation.

Acceleration, it is important to note, is not pre-teaching. Rather, these are captivating experiences to imbed prior knowledge and intellectual curiosity. In essence, educators provide just enough prior knowledge and just-in-time remediation to enable students to latch on to new learning. These are small experiences timewise and can be inserted into various scheduling situations. (When can acceleration take place? See Chapter Three.)

Imagine the change possible when a student who has grown accustomed to not having the right answer suddenly feels newfound confidence in their response? Imagine the change in self-efficacy when teachers and classmates respond positively to those answers. Repeatedly, educators report that the first change they observe when transitioning to acceleration is an increase in student engagement and motivation. In one school in which I consulted; core teachers actually had to engage in gentle conversations with their acceleration students about not dominating class discussions. These learners exhibited such enthusiasm to demonstrate their expertise—to be the ones with the hands up—that they now required guidance on letting others share. One teacher grabbed me after a session and joked, "My acceleration students are acting like "know it alls" now.

The positive change in student motivation and self-efficacy is important. Learners with higher self-efficacy tend to persevere longer, work harder, and participate more readily (Schunk & Meese, 2006). Self-efficacious learners overcome obstacles more effectively and achieve at higher levels. In addition, they are typically more optimistic about school. (Usher & Pajares, 2008). And the changes are authentic—they are doing better in class, and they know it. This observable improvement is welcomed and helpful, but this new confidence must also translate into an increase in academic achievement. What is it about prior knowledge that can move learners so readily?

## THE POWER OF PRIOR KNOWLEDGE

What we know about learning is that one of the key indicators of how effectively a student will learn a concept today is what they already know about the content. By increasing background knowledge by one standard deviation, a student can rise from the 50TH percentile to the 75%. A lack of prior knowledge in this same student could result in a drop from the 50TH percentile to the 25TH percentile (Marzano, 2004).

These academic experiences upon which students draw for new learning must be stored in their permanent memories to be retrieved. For learners experiencing academic decline, they might have missed some pieces the first time around, or the information was forgotten. The reality is that it is very difficult to learn something new without prior knowledge. On the other hand, the presence of prior knowledge makes learning much easier, and even faster. The good news is that students do not need a lot of it—even a foundational amount is helpful. Students exert more effort and pay greater attention when they know a little bit about something (Hattie & Yates, 2014). This critical information about how new learning relies so heavily on the presence of prior knowledge provides a hopeful path for students. Acceleration, therefore, provides this fresh start for new learning by utilizing about 80% of the time developing prior knowledge to jumpstart successful new learning.

The presence of prior knowledge makes learning something new significantly easier. Conversely, the absence of background knowledge makes learning more challenging. For example, imagine arriving to class and hearing this: "Students: please select one of the following to demonstrate in teams today: a nollie, the wallride, an axle stall, or a blunt fakie." A look of confusion—perhaps even desperation—might emerge. But a few students will know that these are skateboarding tricks. Those learners are more likely to raise their hands with enthusiasm and get going. This demonstrates the reality of prior knowledge—a learner in one desk possesses enough prior knowledge to latch on to new learning while a student nearby might not. Some have visited Gettysburg, others have constructed fences, some talk about baseball statistics over the kitchen table, and others tinker with car engines. All valuable prior knowledge, but not all of it relates to the academic tasks at hand. The math lesson today might require words like models, scale, proportion, and dimensions. Which students are connecting to new learning...and which ones would benefit from prior knowledge before this lesson?

Prior knowledge is a critical element in comprehending text. One reader might sail through a passage, while confusion or frustration simmers in other. For example, give the simple passage in the box below a read:

---

**YOUR TURN:**

Read this short passage.

*"It's normal to question your strategies for no trump contracts. My advice is to think about the auction. Look at the opening lead of the robot as well. Also, consider how many definite winners you have. As usual, set up your best suit."*

What is this about?

Circle words that either supported your comprehension...or served as barriers.

---

The passage above is about online contract bridge. Individuals who play card games might have had some inkling, seeing familiar words like trump, suit, and lead. Contracts and auctions are more specific to the card game of bridge. For bridge players, reading comprehension was probably stellar. For readers who do not have background knowledge in playing cards at all, this might have been a frustrating passage. The words themselves are not particularly difficult; rather, the presence of prior knowledge impacted reading comprehension. As with most passages, words have different meanings, including suit, trump, lead, and robot. Readers attach prior knowledge to the text in front of them—was this a misfire or a success?

## PRIOR KNOWLEDGE, PREREQUISITE SKILLS, AND VOCABULARY

An encouraging component of prior knowledge is that even surface level knowledge works well (Marzano, 2004). With time constraints, this is important. Acceleration is not a deep dive. If extra time has been allotted for acceleration, this component is not the mastery class—that is the domain of the core class. For example, students might go on a scavenger hunt for area and perimeter in the acceleration class to imbed prior knowledge for a new unit in the core class. Before embarking on the study of the Earth's crust, mantle, and core, acceleration learners might examine hard boiled eggs as an introduction. Students might create flags on toothpicks to introduce the vocabulary. Vocabulary and prior knowledge are intricately connected. Having said that, passive vocabulary activities, such as definitions, should be minimized.

What experiences would develop prior knowledge just before new learning? Using the suggestions below—or learning targets of your choice—jot down ideas for acceleration tasks that would develop prior knowledge just in time for new learning.

## YOUR TURN:

Select one or more of the targets below. What background knowledge experiences would serve to accelerate new learning? (Ideas below list.)

Learning Targets:

- Demonstrate knowledge of literary genres.

- Interpret the arrangement of the Periodic Table.

- Locate, compare, and order integers and rational numbers on a number line.

- Analyze plot elements, including foreshadowing and suspense.

- Analyze causes of the World War I.

Examples: sorts, videos, scavenger hunt, read aloud, real-world problems, photos, primary documents, similar readings, newspaper articles, games.

## SUMMARY

The key purposes of this chapter have been to articulate:

- The differences between acceleration and remediation
- A rationale for acceleration
- The powerful connection between background knowledge and new learning
- The mission of acceleration, which is for students to learn new concepts on pace with their peers
- The value of just-in-time remediation, in which prerequisite skills that might be missing or forgotten are advanced into the context of new learning

In the following "Your Turn," compare and contrast acceleration with traditional remediation. Next, consider the potential impact of the two approaches. Reminder: There is a remedial component within acceleration, but missing skills are distributed throughout units where they will be applied.

---

*Core refers to the class in which students currently require support. Often referred to as "Tier 1," acceleration can also be employed for advanced courses.

# YOUR TURN:

Below is comparison of two models: Acceleration and Remediation. Personalize this with notes for your school/district.

| *Acceleration* | *Remediation* | *Our Students* |
|---|---|---|
| What students CAN do. | Deficit based. | |
| Tactical, just-in-time review | Laundry list of gaps. | |
| Future-driven; fresh start | Past failures/gaps | |
| Builds academic confidence | Backwards movement | |
| Increases engagement & curiosity | Out of context | |
| Prior knowledge imbedded | Lack of relevance | |

# 3
## GETTING STARTED

Moving from a traditional remedial model to an acceleration approach is a change in instructional mindset. Acceleration is a strength-based plan that is forward-moving, but with pragmatic attention to critical missing pieces that get folded into new learning for success today. This strength-based path rests on the critical connection between prior knowledge and new learning and the understanding that remediation just in time—in the context of helping students learn something new—supports academic success.

Acceleration also has a nuts and bolt component, including scheduling, staffing, and communication. Before reading this chapter, reflect on your current thinking. Either individually or as a group, jot down ideas in the box below. At the end of the chapter, revisit your responses and adjust accordingly. What changes will strengthen your acceleration program?

The process of acceleration requires planning, collaboration, and ongoing refinement. And sometimes, it takes innovative thinking, especially for scheduling. One of the first issues pondered is how to allocate time to accelerate students. Prior knowledge, as discussed in Chapter Two, significantly enhances new learning. Scaffolding forward and remediation just in time, the other pieces to acceleration, proactively revisit just the skills essential to the new concepts. The good news is that learners do not need extensive background knowledge—just enough to build upon.

One of the biggest instructional challenges acceleration teachers contend with is how to move forward when students have significant deficits. In my work, I advocate for an 80-20 model—80% forward and 20% backward. The learning target is the new one, not one from two years ago. The gaps revisited are just those that are critical to learning the new target. There are days when there will be more remediation, simply because the new target requires it. Other learning targets have no prerequisites, so those sessions may be all forward movement. In addition, there are times when students simply need more support. The 80-20 model is a guide to resist the gravitational pull to always remediate.

So, what might that time look like? The following are some ideas for scheduling time for acceleration.

## WHEN TO ACCELERATE

Incorporating a zero period is one option. With this approach, a short time is allotted prior to the first class. *All* students attend a variety of enrichment or acceleration options. Some might attend math, others language arts or science. The strength of this approach is that learners often have their own core teachers. These educators already have their lessons ready to go for the day and can provide laser-like acceleration to prepare students.

## YOUR TURN:

Anticipation Guide

| | |
|---|---|
| **Who?** Which students will benefit from acceleration? What teacher traits best match students' needs? | |
| **What?** What subject(s) will be accelerated? What if students need support in multiple courses? | |
| **When?** What time can be carved out? Scheduling issues? | |
| **Why? How?** What is the mission? What outcomes will be realized? What will instruction look like? What gauges will determine success? | |

In one situation I observed, students advanced so well that they became classroom leaders during the core class. The time allocated was only about twenty-five minutes, but it was highly focused instruction. Teachers made a tacit deal with students: "In exchange for briefly reviewing critical past skills, you are going to have the opportunity to jump ahead of the other learners." The principal more explicitly explained to students that they were going to be provided an opportunity to learn things ahead of the rest of the class. In exchange, however, she also articulated the importance of demonstrating leadership behaviors during the core class. This demonstrates the change of mindset in acceleration—from plausible remedial stagnation to a fresh academic (and sometimes behavioral) start.

A caveat for the zero period, however, is that these sessions can inadvertently turn into homework help. This is an understandable dilemma. Some of the students who are underachieving during the day with imbedded support might also be having difficulty at night with independent homework. One resolution is to initially designate some time for homework help—probably in the beginning. Why? Support on pressing homework issues first can reduce students' stress—they are understandably worried about it and may have difficulty moving forward until concerns are alleviated. For example, ask students to write on a sticky note two problems that were the most challenging. When the buzzer sounds, switch to "Let's look at what you'll be learning later today." Gradually transition to more acceleration time so that learners are prepared for new learning and less homework help is required. A similar situation might occur for an upcoming exam—if students are anxious about a test today, address and support those urgent efforts, but also jump out strong accelerating the upcoming learning target. A final note on zero periods: as progress is realized, students can switch to another offering. So, if they are doing well in math now, perhaps they'd enjoy science acceleration?

Tutoring is another acceleration avenue. Typically held before and/or after school, this can be for select students or open to all. The tutor may not be the core teacher. If the tutor is a different educator, there needs to be an ongoing communication channel. In large schools, tutors often provide support for several teachers. Therefore, it is important that core teachers adhere to pacing guidelines. Learners do better when prior knowledge and scaffolding are tightly attached to new content being presented—with minimum lag time. When core teachers vary too much on pacing, this poses a challenge for the acceleration teacher. The accelerator may have to then jump farther ahead to accommodate for this variance in pacing. A concise table for communication between general education teachers and tutors might include:

- Learning Target to Accelerate
- Key Vocabulary
- Most Urgent Prerequisite Skills
- Timeline.

In my experience, sharing entire lesson plans is an excessive amount for the acceleration partner to digest. Tutoring might be for a shorter timeline, as opposed to a zero period, which typically extends for a grading period, a semester, or even a year. Having said that, my experience has been that tutoring time can provide a much-needed acceleration boost in academic achievement for students.

The double dose is a familiar model in schools, particularly secondary. Select students attend an additional support class alongside the core class. One advantage to this model is time, which is typically the length of a normal class. Many times, the double dose teacher is not the same as their core teacher; therefore, collaboration is essential. In larger schools, planning periods might not be aligned, necessitating a format for communication. As with tutoring, the acceleration person in the double dose might interface with multiple educators; therefore, curriculum pacing is important. In addition, the acceleration teacher may need to have mastery of content in multiple grades or courses. In several particularly effective situations I have observed, the double dose educator's classroom was situated in the middle of the department. In addition to more formal communication, hallway conversations were ongoing, about both the curriculum and progress. In addition, students had the support of two different teachers with different instructional methods.

An innovate approach to acceleration is detailed in a journal article in which Montreal teachers describe their journey from remediation to acceleration. (I spent time working with this staff as part of their planning.) The school began by providing acceleration during lunch. Students also had an option to stay after school. The purpose for the change in direction was a realization that the remedial approach in their school brought with it a decline in the morale of their children. Learners were expending effort, but the remedial work children were doing bore no resemblance to the current curriculum—they were not gaining traction. In their new acceleration approach, students had choices of offerings, groups in reading and math were small, and they did not attend acceleration every day. These teachers utilized hands-on, engaging tasks with a focus on vocabulary. Their positive results and commentary are documented in the article. In addition to a rise in achievement, they discuss the increase in confidence and participation. Note: The journal article is in English; the cover is in French. https://fr.calameo.com/read/0018988804de933eb6e8e4

Zero periods, tutoring, double dose, lunch and learn: what are other ideas? Some schedules have flex times built into schedules; others might utilize homeroom time. Saturday school is an option in some districts. In one elementary school, they simply could not carve out any time for acceleration. Their building focus was math, and they decided to accelerate every student during the final minutes of the day. Grade-level math leaders developed acceleration ideas to imbed prior knowledge for the next day's math lessons. Rather than passively wait on buses at the end of the day, they ended with dynamic math activities.

A scheduling question that arises is instructional timing between acceleration and general education. Multiple exposures of information within no more than a two-day time period boost learning. (Marzano, 2004). This adds credence to the models in which teaching is tightly interwoven with core instruction, such as the zero period, tutoring, double does, and the Montreal work. Students engage in rich opportunities that immerse them in the concept. Acceleration provides the background knowledge first, and the core learning experiences add to it. Therefore, in scheduling, it is helpful to avoid too long of a lag time between acceleration and core classes.

## WHAT IF THERE IS NO TIME?

A designated time for acceleration is ideal. But there are situations in which that is not possible. In that case, acceleration practices are implemented robustly within core instruction. Some of the same strategies employed during a separate acceleration time work beautifully in the opening minutes. Foldables on symmetry or photographs of trench warfare serve to build prior knowledge for all students. A carousel walk with different kinds of rocks to examine and classify make compelling openers. A lab demonstrating transparent, opaque, and translucent instill background knowledge and vocabulary. Without extra time for acceleration, strategies employed during core instruction are even more critical. The open minutes serve as a condensed version of what acceleration might include.

```
YOUR TURN:


What are advantages of students having the same teacher for both acceleration and core
classes?



What are advantages of having an educator *other* than the core teacher being the
accelerator?
```

Stations are another vehicle for imbedding prior knowledge. Consider designating one station for tomorrow's topic. Picture books, videos, and real-world examples are viable options. In addition, a different type of acceleration homework—tasks that prepare learners for tomorrow's concepts—can boost prior knowledge. "Find five things in your house with circumference tonight." Or "Draw a grid of your neighborhood this evening." Or "Watch this short video on Edgar Allan Poe tonight."

Scaffolding prerequisite skills or vocabulary is essential within core instruction. This is true with or without additional acceleration time. Anchor charts, bookmarks, pictures of vocabulary, cheat sheets: these devices serve as bridges to new learning.

## WHO WILL TEACH THEM?

Academically vulnerable learners need special teachers with distinct traits to help them navigate upwards. Be it during acceleration or the core class, teacher selection is vitally important. Academic self-confidence rises with genuine successes, even small ones. Success increases self-efficacy; frequent failures diminish it. Self-efficacy is built through real accomplishments, not prizes. The more they realize authentic success, the harder they will work. For some, however, their history of failure brings hesitancy to keep trying. If they try and realize failure again, task withdrawal might ensue. As students get older, they know when praise or commendations are genuine. They are mindful that teachers are hovering around their desks more than others. They know they are behind.

An underpinning of acceleration is this belief: All students want to be successful. Acceleration utilizes research about prior knowledge, vocabulary, scaffolding, formative assessment, and hands-on captivating learning to spark academic success. But it also relies upon the beliefs of educators selected to work with these children. And success of the acceleration program relies heavily on the instructional toolkits educators bring into the classroom, as well as their own professional self-efficacy and personal philosophies about students who have gotten behind. The selection of educators will influence the effectiveness of these efforts. The initial uptick in motivation that often occurs with acceleration is important for new learning, but these students must make up academic ground.

In short, a teacher having a tough year is probably not the best fit to work with students who are also experiencing a rough patch. That combination will bring predictable outcomes. Why? Some fascinating research reveals that there is a connection between the self-efficacy of the teacher and the achievement of the students in the classroom (Hoy & Davis, 2006).

What does a self-efficacious teacher look like? They are probably the top teachers in the building. These educators are the planners and organizers who are highly enthusiastic about their work (Hoy & Davis, 2006). Open to new ideas about teaching, these are the teachers who will try new things when a path is not working, and they minimize lecturing in class. They tend to incorporate inquiry and small group work. These professionals are less critical when students make mistakes and put more effort into learners who haven't gotten the hang of something. These teachers likely have student-centered learning as their mainstay and are even less controlling about classroom discipline. And they likely feel confident in their subject matter, which contributes to their professional self-efficacy. (Hoy & Davis, 2006).

Furthermore, teachers selected for these positions are intrinsically motivated themselves. They set goals for themselves and their students. They are adept at picking strategies that meet students' needs. And they immerse students in the content—they dig in and spend time on the content. Their high degree of content expertise enables them to answer any question, provide growth feedback, and reteach effectively (Hoy & Davis, 2006). Mastery of content is important, especially with schedules in which they teach multiple grades or subjects. These masterful teachers have high expectations for these learners. They ask challenging questions, but often give more response time to answer. Their actions communicate to their class that they are indeed genuinely able to meet these high expectations. And these educators tend to provide choices of work and build student autonomy, a critical factor in motivation (Hoy & Davis, 2006).

The best candidates for working with learners who need to move quickly are often the dynamos in the building. One caveat, however: Some educators might be of the mindset that negative behaviors automatically follow struggling learners. Of course, students who are in a failure cycle might be more likely to exhibit unproductive behaviors, such as withdrawing from tasks. Caution must be exercised in placing those expectation on these learners. Why? That can lead to "sit-n-git" work that exacerbates reluctance to learning. In a misguided effort to limit off-task behaviors, there is a tendency to relegate struggling learners to seat work. This can keep learners in the same cycle as the past, rather than changing the course of their futures.

---

YOUR TURN:

Draw an outline of a teacher. Select adjectives that describe the best fit for acceleration students.

---

## OTHER NUTS & BOLTS ISSUES

How do we mathematically grade acceleration? Perhaps the question posed should be, "Why in the world would we assign a grade for acceleration?" The reality is, in situations such as a double dose, grades are sometimes required. In my experience, clarification about the purpose of acceleration at the start is helpful. Acceleration is a formative process. It is tightly connected to their progress in the core class, not a separate track. If a grade is required—and this is based solely on my experience—the grade in acceleration tends to be higher than the one received in their core class. They are typically not spending critical time on summative assessments during acceleration—those exams are more likely the domain of the core class. Therefore, if a student has a B in acceleration but a C- in Algebra, this might understandably cause confusion. A parent might ask simply, "Is my child doing better in math or not?" Communication to parents at the start might include the purpose of acceleration and how the assessment measures differ.

Another way to explain the process of acceleration to stakeholders is this: The core class is the mastery class. Acceleration provides support to build that mastery. The two classes work together, but grades taken in acceleration are small in scale and formative in nature. A formative assessment in acceleration resembles three problems on a sticky note. But an assessment in the core class likely has twenty in-depth problems presented as a weekly exam.

There will be children who are struggling in more than one course. Reading impacts every subject, and both math and reading impact science. There are students who begin underperforming across the board due to their low morale or self-efficacy at school. Sometimes, the entire school has a focus for improvement, such as math. Other times, these decisions are made due to scheduling or staffing. In my secondary acceleration class, students were failing multiple courses. I simply asked them to pick two subjects they would most like to improve in. It was a consensus for them—math and science. I soon discovered that reading and vocabulary were the main issues in science. Therefore, the acceleration lessons in math looked different than the ones constructed for science.

What do we call this class? It matters. The "remedial" tag is not helpful for a fresh start. In fact, it has a punitive ring to it. Parents, students, teachers, and administrators all know that these learners have missed some things—it is not helpful to attach labels to them. It can simply be called acceleration. One school calls it Fast Lane. Some create something catchy with the mascot, like "Mustang Time."

## SUMMARY

The purpose of this chapter is to explore ideas for getting started with acceleration. When will the acceleration class occur? What schedule works for learners in our building? The second piece is who will teach them? What traits do some educators possess that make them more likely to be successful with academically vulnerable learners? Revisit the anticipation guide in the opening. What refinements will you make?

---

### YOUR TURN:

Planning for acceleration requires reflection and innovative thinking. Below is a quick check of your progress:

1. Our acceleration class will be called:

2. Our mission:

3. Students:

4. Teachers:

5. Grading (if needed):

6. Schedule:

7. Communication:

8. How we will know acceleration is working:

---

# 4
## MOVING FORWARD WITH STUDENTS WHO ARE BEHIND

FRACTIONS, DECIMALS, AND place value. Surface area, perimeter, and slope. Onomatopoeia, personification, and alliteration. What's the difference in theme, tone, and mood? Is that a translation, dilation, or a rotation? Adjectives, prepositions, and adverbs. Vacuoles and cytoplasm. Au for gold, Fe for iron and K for potassium. Facts, formulas, and rules.

As the days, weeks, and years go by, the list grows. Some students adeptly store information for later retrieval from long term memory. For others, this proves more challenging. These deficits make new learning more difficult. Missing pieces slow students down, increase errors, and understandably cause frustration. but it doesn't have to be that way.

The purpose of scaffolding, the process of utilizing tactical supports to elevate learning, is to help students learn something new. Prerequisite skills are important—and students are still working on them—but now in the context of grasping the new target. Scaffolding acknowledges that the educational journey is a long one and that things sometimes get missed, remain murky, or simply forgotten along the way. In the acceleration model, teachers provide remediation just in time—right when students need the prerequisite skills. In an entirely remedial model, pieces are typically taught in a random sequence with little bearing on today's targets. In acceleration, learners apply these prerequisites in real time when they are most valuable. Learning is easier when it's in context and students can realize success from their efforts. The mission of acceleration is clear: success today on new targets.

Scaffolding provides a hopeful path for students with deficits. When hearing that today's lesson depends on past success with fractions, some are likely thinking, "I'm sunk on this new stuff too since I'm not good at fractions" With scaffolding supports, the message we are striving for is "Whew! Here's something helpful on fractions so that I have a shot at math today." And instead of "Everyone should have their perfect squares memorized by now," the acceleration message is "Keep working on memorizing perfect squares. In the meantime, there's a cheat sheet to tape into your notebooks while you're getting there."

Scaffolding moves learning forward. Rather than a panicked feeling of "I'm terrible at negative numbers," they have a temporary life raft. Anxiety dissipates, and their brains can better focus on learning something new, rather than a frantic search for the missing pieces.

But scaffolding is meant to be reduced, or faded, as observations warrant. In the same way that a youngster first hits a baseball off of a T, the goal is for them to eventually hit a pitched ball. The duration and extent of scaffolding vary by learner and situation. There is a balance between supporting new learning and developing an over reliance on scaffolding. Sometimes, this can be as seamless as, "Let's all try one problem without looking at the anchor chart now."

## SCAFFOLDING FORWARD

Scaffolding is an umbrella term for strategies that support learners in reaching higher goals. Teachers instinctively scaffold throughout the day, by modeling additional problems, displaying a sample project from a previous class, or chunking instructions. For our purposes here, these are tangible devices that can be held, drawn on, highlighted, folded, taped into notebooks, or anchored on the walls. They can be digital or paper but are readily accessible. These devices are quick reference guides of things forgotten, missed, or misunderstood. They are a quick dip back in order to move forward.

Scaffolding in the acceleration model is proactive and moves learning forward. Scaffolding devices can often be prepared in advance of new learning. But scaffolding in acceleration is also judicious—over-scaffolding should be avoided. For example, if a learner knows all of her multiplication tables except sevens and eights, those two are made available. In addition, as a general rule, students do well with having just what they need at the time, rather than an entire packet or file of scaffolding devices.

Shoring up critical prerequisite skills and/or urgent vocabulary is approximately 20% of the acceleration model. This time suggestion is more of a mental guide than an actual allotment of instructional time. There are units in which no prerequisite skills are in play and others where more time is required. The gravitation tendency to remediate a lengthy list of deficits can pull instruction back and back. The 80-20 model is a reminder that success today on new targets is the mission. What this might look like during acceleration class is three stations: two for the new target and one remediation station with additional practice and feedback. (The feedback may simply be an answer key.) That one remediation station, however, is for prerequisite skills needed for the new target.

## SCAFFOLDING DEVICES

Scaffolding can be as simple as pre-annotating text with synonyms of unfamiliar words. This supports more confident reading, especially when coupled with hearing the words pronounced during acceleration time. "Unsure" next to ambiguous or "no backbone" adjacent to invertebrate are examples. Annotation in math word problems alerts students to operation signal words, such as "left over" or "remain" for subtraction. A number line taped on tables, key words in home languages, or steps to using a calculator are other examples of scaffolding that move learning forward. Similarly, a simple sticky note with "PEMDAS" for the order of operations provides just the right support for success in class today—they have what they need to move forward. Likewise, a sticky note with examples of points of view just before the core language arts class instills confidence and just enough prior knowledge to learn something new...right on pace with peers.

Below are other examples of scaffolding devices to fold into new learning. These are reference devices that serve as bridges to support grasping new concepts. Without these, some students' brains expend energy searching for missing pieces, rather than focusing on instruction.

Other learners might just shut down right from the start. Scaffolding devices remove barriers to learning something new.

**Bookmarks.** Handy, small, unobtrusive, and to-the-point, bookmarks provide a handy reference of just what's needed. Perfect for memory-related items, students tape them into their agendas or tuck them in their books. Other times, these can be simply secured on desks or provided to everyone digitally or with paper. Capitalization and comma rules, verb conjugations, parts of speech, multiplication tables, perfect squares, properties, formulas, and science prefixes are examples of things suitable for bookmarks. The effective use of bookmarks enables students to practice more accurately. Symbols for inequalities referenced on a bookmark, for example, support their memory during practice. As they become more proficient, reliance diminishes. The bookmark below serves as a quick reminder of prefixes for the number of atoms in an element.

| Number of Atoms | Prefix | Number of Atoms | Prefix |
|---|---|---|---|
| 1 | mono | 6 | hexa |
| 2 | di | 7 | hepta |
| 3 | tri | 8 | octa |
| 4 | tetra | 9 | nona |
| 5 | penta | 10 | deca |

**Cheat sheets.** Items requiring more explanation or room fit nicely into cheat sheets. Figurative language examples fit into this category, as well as types of sentences and point of view. Types of lines, as well as types of angles and triangles work well as cheat sheets. Need examples of hooks for writing or narrative endings? Here are ideas. Support in keeping electrical circuits or types of genres straight can be provided on cheat sheets. Similarly, parts of a cell or types of energy. Active versus passive verbs? A bookmark or cheat sheet would be appropriate. Metric conversions? Cheat sheets or anchor charts work well.

The example below could be enhanced with student drawings:

SAMPLE:

Figurative Language Cheat Sheet

| Device | Definition | Example |
|---|---|---|
| Alliteration | Group of words that begin with same sound | David's donuts are delicious. |
| Onomatopoeia | Words that come from sounds they make | Sizzle, honk, boom |
| Personification | Non-human items with human characteristics | The waves called to her. |
| Hyperbole | Obvious exaggeration not meant literally | I have a mountain of homework |

**Steps.** Remember learning to parallel park? The driving instructor articulated clear steps to position the car into that small space. Repeated practice with those steps increased (hopefully!) your proficiency. Similarly, youth basketball coaches provide steps to mastering the layup shot...perhaps with tape on the gym floor. Concept mastery in the classroom for some skills also requires following steps. It takes time to remember all those steps. An adage in math is "Practice Makes Permanent." As learners make sense of the new concept, clearly articulated steps can be helpful in instilling more accurate practice. Simplifying radicals, solving equations, drafting an essay, using a calculator, converting decimals to fractions: clear steps help bridge upward to success. Similarly, a well-executed work sample with highlighted steps demonstrates concrete next steps for learners. Steps provide a clear path to success. Science lab procedures, projects or other involved instructions can be broken into steps for students. And while scaffolding is often for learners with missing pieces, steps typically help all students bring order to an onslaught of information.

**Visuals and graphic organizers.** Often presented as anchor charts on walls, these provide quick glance reminders. Anchors for place value, types of lines, or apostrophe use support learning. The layers of the Earth, planets, atmospheres, 3D figures and angles are very visual. But metric conversions and flow charts also work well as anchors. Learners can snap pictures of these visuals to have at their fingertips. In addition to anchor charts, foldables and organizers support learners in making sense of and bringing structure to new content. Be it parts of systems, types of energy, types of economies, periods of time, or traits of triangles—acceleration learners benefit from supports that bring order to large amounts of incoming (or previously taught) information.

The visual below reminds students of signs when multiplying or dividing integers. Students draw a Tic-Tac-Toe board and write negative signs on the diagonal. Then they fill in the other boxes with + signs. As they practice, they can check their work with this device: a positive x a negative = a negative, but a negative x a negative = a positive.

| + | - | - |
|---|---|---|
| - | + | - |
| - | - | + |

**TIP charts**, something I created and outlined in my books, work well as anchors. TIP charts (Term-Info-Picture) provide just the academic vocabulary learners need right now. The "Info" piece is in understandable, everyday language, rather than dictionary definitions. Pictures are one of the most effective ways to learn new words. This is a quick reference guide—learners certainly benefit from deeper dives as the unit develops. TIP charts provide opportunities for multiple exposures and referencing, a critical component of learning new vocabulary.

TIP charts are most effective when words are added one or two at a time with fanfare. When introducing parallel lines, for example, add that one word. Have students repeat the word and write it on the chart. Next, talk about what it means and create a concise classroom definition. Last, ask students what drawing would best fit the word. Are train tracks parallel? The running track on our field? Intersecting lines might be the next added, followed by perpendicular. As lessons continue, remind students to look at their TIP chart as a reminder. Note: For departmentalized classes, the expectation is not to create new TIP charts every class period. Rather, inquire what drawing they would include or additions they might make to the definition.

| Term | Info | Picture |
|---|---|---|
| Intersecting | Lines cross | ✗ |
| Parallel | Lines never cross | ⇉ |

---

### YOUR TURN:

Select a target below or use one of your own. 1) Jot down the prerequisite skills and/or vocabulary required for success on this target. 2) Create a scaffolding device that best supports this new learning.

   a. Round decimals to tenths or hundredths.

   b. Multiply and divide integers.

   c. Determine the area of a triangle.

   d. Distinguish between chemical and physical changes in matter.

   e. Demonstrate the difference between speed, velocity, and acceleration.

   f. Correctly use commas, semicolons, and colons in writing.

   g. Identify homonyms, synonyms, antonyms, denotations, and connotations

---

## BALANCING NEW TARGETS AND GAPS

Scaffolding devices provide quick references for both past gaps and incoming information. But bridging devices are just part of the remediation component during acceleration. Learners are often going to need additional practice time on critical missing pieces.

How can acceleration strike a balance between academic deficits while focusing on new targets? These are big decisions, and effective practice depends on the content and situation. Math standards often have distinct prerequisite skills to be refreshed and scaffolded in the context of the new target. Comprehending dense biology or physics text, on the other hand, relies heavily on vocabulary development. In reading, there are students whose reading levels will make reading upcoming text in grade-level content text frustratingly difficult. For all students, however, developing prior knowledge about the topic and some hands-on work on a few of the most critical vocabulary words will boost reading comprehension. Pre-annotating texts, visuals, picture books, read-alouds, choral reads, videos, and leveled tests can be used to prepare students for the content reading. If students are about to read about reptiles, for example, a museum walk with pictures and videos can provide just enough prior knowledge to enhance new learning.

The planning process for acceleration is a reflective one. It might be helpful to begin by answering this question:

"Students could achieve success on the new target if they just knew _____."

This simple, hopeful question establishes the vision of success on the new target. The table below expands that question out to a unit. Is there some critical background knowledge that might boost new learning? Academic vocabulary that will emerge again—words like congruent, symmetry, or equivalent? Genre, narrative, perspective? Will a long-forgotten math formula be needed in science this week? Again, only the most critical pieces are introduced to support new learning—every blank will not be completed.

| Background Knowledge | Vocabulary | Prerequisite Skills | Target # |
|---|---|---|---|
| | | | 1 |
| | | | 2 |
| | | | 3 |
| | | | 4 |

## WHAT REMEDIATION LOOKS LIKE DURING ACCELERATION

Acceleration is an active learning experience. Station teaching is a logical instructional vehicle for providing active forward movement and just in time remediation. One station might include practice on just the prerequisite skill needed for the new target while the other stations introduce the new concept.

But practice does not necessarily mean work sheets. Students can play cards with partners! Playing cards make learning multi-sensory and collaborative. For example, one student can flip a card and be the x, the other learner the y. Now, together they solve 2x + 4y. Another card game is for one partner to have the red (negative) cards and the other the positive black ones. They flip over cards one at a time and race to multiply the integers.

Cards are just one way to make learning hands-on. Problems can be written on cubes and rolled and solved at one station. For an upcoming target on fractions, each station might include real-world measuring with spoons and cups or dividing actual food. Sorting is a stellar strategy for remediation—learners don't even need a pencil! Instead, they move pieces with their hands while problem-solving with their partner. Students can arrange fractions and models from smallest to largest or match equivalent fractions. Another simple sort is for students to create two stacks– rational and irrational or perimeter or area. In science, two sorting categories might be in play: vertebrates and invertebrates or renewable and nonrenewable. A station might include artistic endeavors as well—sculpting, drawing, or building, for example.

Stations for scaffolding reading might include small pieces of text, accompanied by videos or audio reads. One teacher station might be intertwined for some students needing targeted reading support. In the social studies arena, two stations might be created for upcoming targets, such as a "Leaders During the Cold War" station and "Causes of the Cold War" station. But one station might be teacher led to preview upcoming social studies reading. Science stations might have one part of the respiratory system at each station, with one teacher station to preview upcoming text.

Stations provide immersion in a concept in creative, thoughtful ways. Examples of station tasks include labs, picture books, error analysis, manipulatives, sculpture, art, videos, games, quick writes, sorts, cubes, agree/disagrees, facts/fibs, short reads, or courseware. Of course, stations can also be just some extra practice or tutoring.

Stations are, of course, just one lesson model. A simple museum walk of practice problems can be created with sticky chart paper on the walls. Partners select a marker color, solve the first problem and then rotate around. At the end of the carousel, each team's work is represented by color. Carousels work beautifully for vocabulary development as well. Each sheet has one word. Students create a summary of the word and craft a visual depiction—now they rotate. Students of all ages enjoy writing on boards of any type. In fact, individual white boards for math should be a mainstay for acceleration.

What about courseware? Stations provide an opportunity to use courseware for additional practice on skills. As much as possible, align the courseware assignments with this week's targets. Remediation is more effective when learning is in context, active, captivating and being applied. In addition, a good practice is to weave in white boards or have students work out problems right on their desks alongside the courseware. This makes work more visible for quick feedback. Courseware, like other decisions when working with urgent groups, must be tactical in nature. It is best utilized as one component in a fabulous instructional plan.

In sum: What might the remediation component look like during acceleration? It is blended in with new concepts in a variety of ways. Any while they need practice on missing skills, it is advisable to avoid anything that resembles a worksheet

## OTHER SCAFFOLDING

Examples of scaffolding thus far have been for academic targets. Some learners need more. Students with attention deficits, for example, have distinct characteristics that make long school days challenging for them. Additional memory structures, such as bookmarks and cheat sheets are particularly essential for them. These learners may need additional organizational supports. Agendas, folder systems, ensuring that they have supplies, check-off lists, reminders, and time management apps—these are a few support ideas for this particularly vulnerable group. If a project is underway, these learners require additional organizational strategies—timelines, steps, and help with organizing resources. Movement is a critical component for attention deficit learners. Not only does movement enhance learning—it is also therapeutic for these students. Therefore, standing and/or allowing movement while working can help them sustain their efforts. Breaking work into smaller pieces, shorter assignments, and goal setting are additional strategies that can be offered for these often talented, but sometimes challenging, students.

Students who are trying to master English at the same time they are trying to conquer physics or "The Odyssey" face particular challenges. Many of the devices outlined earlier—bookmarks, steps, cheat sheets, TIP charts, and chunking—are helpful for all students. In addition to those, students in the process of learning English benefit from hearing about the new concept in their home language. During acceleration, one station might include videos in their home language introducing figurative language or the Pythagorean Theorem. TIP charts might include the words in their home language as well. Visuals woven throughout instruction advances learning. Labs, manipulatives in math, and additional modeling support learning. Is it OK for these students to pair up and speak about the content in their home language? Yes!

## THE FLUID NATURE OF SCAFFOLDING AND REMEDIATION

As acceleration unfolds over the course of a unit, there will be times when the core teacher reports that additional clarification, tutoring, or practice is required. This valuable feedback should quickly be incorporated into the lesson. This may look like additional practice during acceleration on the new skill: a pop-up station, white boards, or some carousel practice with a partner. Additional scaffolding devices might be needed, but now for the new concept. This ad hoc addition to instruction serves to prevent new gaps from developing. Again, there will be units in which few prerequisites exist and others with several. Some new content is more complex than others and may require additional support along the way.

Acceleration is tightly connected to core instruction. Both instructional components move forward to serve students. How did acceleration students do in class today? Did they engage in the tasks? Did they ask questions? Did they readily work with a partner? What evidence of learning can be assembled and examined?

While schedules vary for acceleration, the mission remains the same: to support students in learning new concepts today alongside their peers. This mission, while ambitious, relies on the positive dynamic between possessing prior knowledge and learning something new. Prior knowledge lifts reading comprehension levels and enhances engagement. New incoming infor-

---

## YOUR TURN:

On your own or with a group, express how your acceleration model balances missing skills or gaps with learning new concepts.

---

mation latches on to prior knowledge. Intellectual curiosity is higher when background knowledge is present, as well as retention in long-term memory. Without prior knowledge, learning something new is almost insurmountable. What is known is that students are more apt to engage in learning when prior knowledge is present.

Acceleration students have an opportunity to experience mini lessons that prepare them for new core content—to develop just enough background knowledge. These lessons include captivating tasks. They might take pictures of every right triangle in the building and then talk about the word "hypotenuse." Or they might be the only students in the building to learn that the Pythagorean theorem actually dates back to tablets from Babylon, way before Pythagoras was even born. ELA students might engage in a figurative language sort to refresh their memories or play a game in which they try to find figurative language in cartoons. Or they might analyze a poem similar to one they will read in their core classroom. .

Prior knowledge overlaps with academic vocabulary. In fact, it is sometimes difficult to separate the two. Seeing that the word "transversal" is upcoming in geometry, the acceleration class might create a transversal with ribbon and learn that "trans" means across. Acceleration students get a jump start on vocabulary. As a result, the core teacher should observe increased confidence in this area.

A caveat with vocabulary: Engaging learners with two or three words at a time is more productive than long lists of words. Best practices dictate a gradual building with multiple, diverse exposures over time. One or two words today, a third tomorrow, and another word to celebrate and explore the next day. Pictures, games, clay, applause when a vocabulary word is used—these strategies tend to yield better results than copying information down.

Prerequisite skills are another component of prior knowledge. For planning purposes, it might be helpful to view these as memory items, such as parts of speech, comma rules, place value, multiplication tables, or perfect squares. This is the 20% piece and consists of just enough backwards movement to prepare them to go forward with confidence. This is the tradeoff for students: spend a little time on rather nagging skills, such as place value. In exchange, you will have the opportunity to jump ahead of the class on new content.

## SUMMARY

Learners may initially find a topic captivating and jump right in, motivated to learn. And then it happens. They realize they need decimals again. Adverbs...again? Comma rules...again? Their initial enthusiasm dissipates. Their perception of a successful outcome—a key factor in motivation—slides below the positive range. Frustration rises. "Well, I won't be able to do this today." They withdraw from the task. And those still engaged in the activity experience something of a cognitive overload as their brains take off searching for those critical missing pieces. "Which one is the denominator again? I know it's in my brain somewhere..."

The acceleration process anticipates barriers to new learning and tactically lowers them. Yes, in a perfect world they would all remember their multiplication tables. But today in class we are applying them—they need them to learn the new skills. These tangible devices provide a reference on which students rely. Scaffolding can build student autonomy—they have something in their hands upon which they can rely for new learning. Scaffolding reduces mistakes caused by unfinished learning. And as they reference these devices, they are still learning the missing pieces—and it is now in context.

Why scaffold? It supports learning in many ways—four of which are below:

- Students continue working on the learning target.
- Motivation increases.
- Frustration decreases.
- The scaffolding takes over part of the brain's work, thus reducing a learner's cognitive load so they can think about the new learning (Van de Pol, Volman, & Beishuizen, 2010).

How might this look in a real acceleration class? If the core class is about to embark on learning circumference, students in acceleration are introduced to the concept first, perhaps with a slide show of real-world circumference. Next, they use string and jar lids to measure circumference. Circumference might now be written on a TIP chart. Now they take another string and measure diameter and discuss that new word, adding it to the TIP chart. Next, students write the formula for circumference on a sticky note and tuck that in their math books for their "regular" class. Now, they might shore up one prerequisite skill. Finally, they get to practice a couple of foundational problems with circumference.

The following day, the core teacher introduces circumference. The acceleration students now have prior knowledge to learn alongside their classmates. In fact, the hope is that hands go up! What if they still need additional work with circumference? The core teacher alerts the acceleration partner, who weaves additional practice into their next session. The acceleration teacher, however, stays just ahead of the core class's lessons.

What if there is no additional acceleration time? Scaffolding forward is essential in core instruction as well as acceleration. And prior knowledge experiences are valuable in every class-room. However, it is easy to see the advantage of carving out even a small amount of time for acceleration. Acceleration students engage in multiple exposures, practice, scaffolding, and vocabulary introduction prior to their core learning experiences, which can yield significant advantages.

---

# CONFIDENCE CHECK

On a scale of 1-5, rate your confidence. (5= Highly Confident; 1 = Unsure)

1. An effective planning & communication process for acceleration is in place.

    1   2   3   4   5

2. Acceleration instruction is engaging and of high interest.

    1   2   3   4   5

3. Instructional time has a solid balance between moving forward and picking up pieces.

    1   2   3   4   5

4. Scaffolding forward is a strength for both acceleration and core instruction.

    1   2   3   4   5

5. Evidence of student improvement is present.

    1   2   3   4   5

---

# 5
## HOW TO MOTIVATE STUDENTS
## (EVEN THOSE WHO HAVE GIVEN UP)

THE CELL PHONE alarm blasts. No movement. The snooze alarm sounds. Nothing. Parents rouse. Parents rouse again. A reluctant bus ride ensues—back to a school situation that just yesterday did not go well. Struggling learners arrive at the school door with their histories of failure in tow. It cannot be easy for some of these apprehensive students to cross the school threshold again and again. Some are hopeful that today will be different. Others simply want to hide, to avoid tasks that might again lead to disappointment, embarrassment, or even failure. Some continue to engage in homework theatrics—dramatically searching for a sheet of paper they know does not exist. A couple of them, however, fail to arrive with even pencils.

How can teachers and leaders motivate students who are in varying degrees of giving up on school, on themselves, or perhaps even on us? What strategies will get all students expending effort and authentically engaging in their work? To spark your thinking, imagine stopping by the classroom below during a brief learning walk. What instructional elements are present that encourage student motivation? Code your text with an "M" when a motivator exists.

---

### YOUR TURN:

During learning walks, the classroom below was observed. Mark all components that positively impact motivation with an "M."

In preparation for a deep dive into the workings of the stock market, groups create lists of their favorite products—from sneakers to restaurants. They divide these amongst their teammates and search for the companies on the stock market page, jotting down their ticker symbols, price, and percent change. The teacher provides ongoing feedback to the groups and places a check mark on the classroom agenda when they are moving on. A brief mini lesson ensues on market fundamentals. Another checkmark. With great enthusiasm for the content, the teacher explains their next steps: They will take on the role of a portfolio manager. Their mission: to make money for their clients. First decision: to work in groups, pairs, or on your own...First job: visit the companies' websites and gather data.

---

The learning experience above demonstrates the relationship between lesson design, instructional practices, and student motivation. Imbedded, often subtle, elements within lessons and their delivery spark the motivation to learn. What motivators did you select?

## STUDENT AUTONOMY

The lesson above has traits of what are broadly referred to as student-centered learning. Learners selected companies/products of personal interest. Direct instruction was tactically targeted to prepare students for their group and independent work, and it was appropriate in length. And choices were provided, included how to work and companies of interest.

The world of school, one can argue, is largely controlled by adults. To maintain safety and order, much of a student's day is in lock step—dress codes, class times, lunch at 11:51—with few options for student autonomy or decision making. But inside the four walls of the classroom, giving learners more control over how they learn can positively impact motivation and student achievement. In general, teachers who provide opportunities for student autonomy get better results than more teacher-centered classrooms. (Brophy, 2010).

Teacher talk should be targeted and brief. How much teacher expertise is required to be presented or modeled for student understanding is a big decision when crafting lessons. Students need time to explore, process information, research, share ideas, and practice -to make sense of incoming information. In fact, students are at their lowest level of engagement during the times when teachers are doing the talking. Conversely, the highest levels of student engagement exist during labs and collaborative learning. (Yair, 2000).

When active work moves to students' shoulders, teaching is still ongoing. It just looks different. Teachers are now learning alongside students in groups, facilitating a station, looking at developing work, and providing feedback. In my experience, the more rapidly we reasonably move the active learning to students, the higher the engagement. Students need tactical, explicit instruction. They also need captivating experiences and the time to process information, and receive descriptive, growth-oriented feedback.

What we know is that students are less motivated to work in teacher-centered, over managed instructional settings. Motivation increases, however, when students experience some autonomy over their learning. Providing choices throughout learning experiences is a fertile avenue for empowering students. These can be small choices woven into instruction—it could be as simple as letting students make decisions about the order in which they want to complete their work. In math or physics, choices might be given for how students can show their work; for example, some might show their work by writing on their desks with washable markers while others prefer using technology. In science, some students might choose to create a digital flowchart of the circulatory system while others embark on drawing and labeling the system. In reading, students might have three options: read with a partner, on your own, or in the teacher circle. Rather than the entire class reading the same novel, consider implementing literature circles in which students select books based on their own interests. And in math: Here are ten problems—select five that you like.

Choices can enhance motivation for all students, but particularly for vulnerable learners who are struggling at school. School can feel futile, as if they have no personal control over their achievement. Getting to make decisions about tasks—having a little bit of power—can reignite the motivation buried within. Choice is a motivator that belongs in every educator's toolkit.

Menus, or choice boards, advance the practice of incorporating student autonomy. The one below is a vocabulary example. Learners select one task of interest every day– from creating memes to business slogans to designing a piece of jewelry—have some fun with ten new words!

| Day | Choice 1 | Choice 2 | Choice 3 |
|---|---|---|---|
| Monday | Create word art for 3 words. (Ex: Write "plateau" in the shape of a plateau.) | Create a rhyme with 3 of the words that explains what they mean. | Create a mini-crossword puzzle & answer key with the 3 words. |
| Tuesday | Create a compare & contrast chart with 2 of your words. | Write a short news story with 2 of your words. | Create a social media post using any 2 of your words. |
| Wednesday | Design a package label with 2 of the words. | Create a T-Shirt design with 2 of the words. | Create a business slogan with any 2 words. |
| Thursday | Create a meme with 2 of the words. | Create a sports, weather, or fashion headline with 2 of the words. | Incorporate 2 of the words in a sneaker ad. |
| Friday | With your last word, create a website name & explain its meaning. | Use your last word. Design a piece of jewelry Explain its meaning. | Create a video game name with the last word. Explain. |

Another wonderful menu model is a 20-50-80. Particularly effective in math, one row has twenty-point problems, another fifty, and the last eighty. Students mix and match to get a hundred points—learners play a key role in determining their grade today! Some educators enjoy creating menus that resemble those in restaurants, with an appetizer, an entrée, and a dessert. The following government menu is an example of a block menu. Learners circle how they want to demonstrate their understanding and the order in which they complete the work.

## Branches of Government Menu

A block menu is represented below. Instructions: Select one choice from each row for a total possible score of 100.

| Topic | Choice A | Choice B | Choice C | Point Value |
|---|---|---|---|---|
| Who Represents YOU? | Create a short video that explains to citizens of your state who represents them at the federal level. | Create a chart for new voters in your state that shows who represents them at the federal level. | Draw a graphic for a newspaper website that details who represents them in Washington DC and where they are from. | 30 |
| Separation of Powers | Create a foldable or flip chart that details the responsibilities of each branch of government. | Create a graphic organizer that details the responsibilities of each branch of government. | Draw a children's picture book explaining the benefits of the branches of government. | 35 |
| Checks and Balances | Create an original diagram that demonstrates checks and balances between the 3 branches. | Create a power point that explains checks and balances between the 3 branches of government. | Create one page of a textbook/website that explains the concept of checks and balances. | 35 |
| Total Points | | | | /100 |

## VICARIOUS LEARNING EXPERIENCES

In the learning walk example above, the teacher exhibited professional self-efficacy. How? Enthusiasm and confidence in content were present. Learners' self-efficacy increases in the midst of these teachers—students sort of absorb some of their teacher's confidence. Moreover, the lesson tactically moved the most riveting part of the work to students' shoulders. This instructional decision demonstrates a confidence—a high degree of expectation—in the students. The teacher could have presented a slide slow on the stock market and simply told everything to them. Students could have robotically copied notes from the presentation. Rather, the mini lesson provided them with the background knowledge and tools to take the academic plunge on their own. Of course, the teacher provided support (feedback) to advance their progress.

Furthermore, the students had some work time in teams. When students work alongside diligent, persevering peers, their academic efforts tend to rise. Much like going to the gym with a workout partner, we simply try harder. Interesting, vicarious experiences are even more powerful when the models are fellow students rather than teachers. When other learners in the classroom demonstrate traits of self-efficacy, this buoys the confidence of other students. Why? Because they are more like them in terms of age and ability level. Positive examples spread the message to other learners that they can engage successfully in this task as well. (Schunk & Meese, 2006).

Research on vicarious experiences and motivation spotlight some traditional practices often employed with academically vulnerable learners. These students, in an effort to remediate past gaps, are often grouped together, scheduled together, and even pulled out of class together. And while grouping must be tactical—we would never match a Wimbledon champ with a beginning player—flexible grouping can support all learners. A talented artist at each table, an adept keyboarder, an organizer, and a fast reader. One of my favorite methods of grouping is by job title. When students enter, they select color-coded strips with jobs, such as editor, illustrator, and researcher. The blue team, red team, etc. all have equally important jobs to do.

Responsibility to a team is a motivator, even for adults. In tactically constructed team work, students are inherently motivated to rise to the challenge—they do not want to let their team members down. But along the school journey, students who are behind might experience more isolation, less opportunities for team experiences, and more deficit-centered instruction. It is inevitable that they will be grouped or scheduled together at times. Students missing a math credit, for example, will be situated next semester or in summer school with others with the same academic experiences. Exemplary instructional practices, therefore, are critical to their success.

Vicarious experiences boost motivation. "The British Baking Show" features bakers vying for a grand prize. While binge watching this program, I always feel an urge to bake something from scratch. Bread, cookies, cakes, and scones—every time I click another episode to watch my motivation grows. The interesting part is that I have a history of culinary catastrophes. And yet, I'm sure I can do it this time! Watching highly enthusiastic, successful bakers makes me buy obscure ingredients and preheat the oven! Share your favorite vicarious experience below.

---

YOUR TURN:


Reflect upon a time in which a vicarious experience motivated you to try something new or work harder.

---

## VALUABLE, RELEVANT TASKS

Personal autonomy motivates students to engage in their work. Thoughtfully constructed teams and self-efficacious teachers also boost effort and authentic engagement. But lessons can still fall flat if another element is missing—valuable, compelling tasks. The tasks need to be worth taking a risk on. After all, failure may loom. Secondly, the tasks must be worth expending effort. Brains get tired and look for opportunities to rest—the task must be important enough to move from rest to work.

And the tasks must be within the realm of possibilities in terms of success. If they are far too difficult, students will likely withdraw from those tasks at some point. Conversely, tasks that are too simple or unimportant may meet the same fate. And yes, many compliant learners dutifully complete every task at school, even the tedious ones. For students with a history of academic failure, however, the value of the tasks created is keenly important. Captivating, relevant, important tasks are more worth the risk of failure.

In fact, the two elements needed to most fully engage students are high value tasks accompanied by individual self-confidence. Both elements are critical—even self-confident learners tend to evade tasks that are boring, tedious, or lack personal relevance. Task rejection- the bottom tier of engagement—is most apt to occur when tasks have both low value and students lack confidence in their potential success. (Hansen, 1989.) Relevant, enthralling tasks have the power to significantly boost student engagement. For students in an academic lull, the tasks placed in front of them are particularly important.

In the situation above, the stock market has a high level of inherent value to many students. Students can make money with businesses of interest. Granted, learning about the stock market is a real world, interesting learning target. Other targets require more creative thinking during lesson planning. World history, Greek mythology, geometry theorems—how can tweaks to lessons transform standards into captivating, relevant tasks?

To increase the value of tasks and thus motivation, ideas to consider include:

- Transform part of the lesson to a hands-on lab. Students can experiment, explore, or build. From geometry constructions to maps to measuring cups to physics, labs tend to yield higher motivation.
- Ask students to make a case or take a stand based on what they learn during the task. A simple masked tape line across the room can be utilized. Are students For or Against? Do they agree or disagree? Four corners is another popular forum-builder. In a reading lesson, for example, each corner has signs posted with characters' names. Students respond to a question by moving to a corner and conversing with like-minded readers. With which character would you most like to have dinner? Which character is the most misunderstood?
- Elevate problem-solving. A local business needs help to make a profit, a local agency needs legal advice. Thinking at a higher level can inspire learning! Students often enjoy error analysis. Where are the math errors? Where did the reasoning break down?
- Incorporate choices in reading to boost motivation.
- Make it hands-on. Sorts, math manipulatives, measuring devices, dividing cookies. Touch adds another sensory element to learning.
- Incorporate local examples—city map, malls, local election returns with percentages, restaurants in the area, energy expended by the school, cafeteria selections, sports
- Include authentic writing—emails to the mayor, editorials, online reviews, blogs

## GOAL SETTING

In the classroom observed above, an agenda was utilized to both demonstrate the big picture of the lesson and individual components to be completed. Agendas typically list lesson components, such as the opener, tasks students will complete during the middle section, and the close. Agendas support predictability, a sense of forward movement, and reaching classroom goals. Many teachers place the learning target at the top of the agenda, either as an essential question or "I Can" statement. It feels good to check off boxes when tasks are completed. This straightforward, methodical tool also lets students know what to expect today—no curveballs are coming.

Setting goals is a motivational technique broadly used in business, sports, finance, and in our personal lives. In general terms, goals should be attainable, measurable, and on a timeline. It is difficult to make real progress without goals or expectations clearly established. In the world of education, students move from subject to subject, hour to hour. School can feel like a blurry place in which learners save files or place papers in bins. But what are we doing? How do the tasks connect? What does success look like?

Setting goals with students is critical for success. The proverbial essential question posted on a wall next to the flag lacks the components of clear, reachable, timely goals. The example below starts with the overarching unit standard and then lists learning targets that will enable proficiency of the standard. This approach does not list tasks to be completed; rather, the targets to be mastered. The overall unit goal (standard) is listed, followed by individual targets.

**I can use models and diagrams to explain the Pythagorean Theorem.**

- I can determine the square root of a number.
- I can determine the area of squares.
- I can describe the characteristics of a right triangle.
- I can solve equations.
- I can write equations.

Goals in the above example have the benefit of clearly demonstrating what a learner must demonstrate for success on this standard. If utilizing portfolios, learners arrange their work—either digitally or with paper—by the targets. Assessments connect to targets, so that grading is transparent. This approach also demonstrates to students the part to the whole, and the relationship between yesterday's work, today's tasks and tomorrow—a progression of learning. In addition, this unit approach visualizes that by reaching proximal goals every day, the end goal—the standard—can be achieved.

An enhancement of the list approach above is what I refer to in my books as "Standards Walls." Rather than a list, a concept map is created with the unit standard in the center and targets arranged around the center. This visual road map provides drawing space to support learning and room to post student work. In the example above, examples of square roots could be colorfully added, as well as right triangles and the area of squares. In addition, synonyms next to vocabulary, such as determine and area. Progress is also shown on these with dramatic check marks when the class is ready to move on. A bonus to the concept map approach is that visual organizers have a proven track record of enhancing memory.

Goal setting is fundamental to success in both the core class and acceleration. Clear goals take the murky out of learning and provide a path for success. The ones discussed thus far, however, are for the entire class. Students also benefit from setting and meeting individual goals. Leaners who have experienced academic failure especially need to reach goals. Self-efficacy is built and renewed from genuine academic accomplishment. In other words, they need to get a couple of math problems right or do a solid job on determining the main idea of a paragraph.

Proximal goals for struggling learners may need to be broken down into smaller parts. Rather than tackle the entire writing process, goals might be a) locate three quotes that would kick off the paper. b) Select one quote. c) Write your introductory paragraph. d) Preview what is coming. In reading, students might place a sticky flag as a goal for the day. In math, one problem on a sticky note or white board is our starting goal. Now, three problems on your own paper.

Goals typically have times attached for completion, such as six minutes for the opener or ten minutes per station. Many teachers utilize timers to keep the appropriate pace for each lesson segment. Generally speaking, timers are a good teaching practice. For some learners, however, the moving timer can exacerbate frustration. Our more deliberate readers, for example, may need an extra minute to complete the reading at the station. And many math learners stop working when members of their team have already completed the problems. They could be equally successful—if they just had two more minutes.

A potential solution is to let students know beforehand that the timer is a guide, not a locked in time. Let their progress be the guide. Announce that bonus time has been awarded due to the hard work being witnessed. Conversely, turn the timer off early as needed. For stations that include text, consider having leveled text or starring the most important passages. Explain to students that the starred passages are the most critical, to help them manage time. Another solution: when working in stations, enable students to revisit stations for a few minutes to finish up.

---

## YOUR TURN:

In both acceleration and core classrooms, describe how clear goals will be articulated.

---

## ONGOING FEEDBACK

Intricately related to goal setting is ongoing descriptive feedback to reach those goals. Performance teachers—sports, music, art, culinary arts—have a distinct advantage in the feedback arena. A tennis coach immediately sees where a serve lands and the speed and spin of the ball. Culinary arts teachers smell the burning bacon and touch the sifted flour. And music teachers will halt a practice within seconds when the clarinets are off key. The academic classroom is different. Tilted computer screens and worksheets with arms draped over them can make seeing work a challenge. And how many students are actually reading that assigned passage?

The critical point is this: feedback begins with students' visible work. Their work is our gauge for feedback. What part of the target are they getting? Where did their math break down? What support might they need? What encouragement might be provided? Performance teachers see, hear, and taste student work. Academic teachers have to practically mine for that ongoing data. And some of our reluctant learners understandably might not want to share their writing, reading, or math.

Soft, ungraded formative practices work well with reluctant learners to get them to share what they know. Ongoing soft assessments with feedback can crescendo to success on summative ones. On a sticky note, ask students to do just one problem and write their names on the back. Now, splash those on the board when you have finished. Provide quick feedback to each student on that one problem. Explain how if they correct just this one little thing their answer will be perfect. Now, proudly put it on the board again. Feels great to be successful. Now, try one on a white board. Or, have students carousel with one or two problems per station. Quick, descriptive feedback as we go to progress. Now, do three just like that on paper or utilizing courseware.

The role of feedback in a learner's progress is astounding. Students situated in classrooms rich in formative assessments can learn twice as fast as classrooms lacking in this piece. (Black & William, 98) This news is hugely important for our academically weaker students—they can learn much faster with formative assessments and feedback. These ungraded assessments combined with descriptive feedback are indeed one of most vital tools in moving students upward...and in making up some time.

## SOME PRINCIPLES OF PROVIDING FEEDBACK TO MOTIVATE STUDENTS AND MOVE LEARNING INCLUDE:

- **Tightly connect feedback to progress on the learning target.** Present tangible ideas on how performance can be improved quickly. Work a problem with them, provide steps, or provide sample work as guidance. Commend areas that are correct—even if it is simply getting off to a good start.

- **Provide feedback as quickly and as frequently as possible.** This is true especially when a concept is new and with academically vulnerable learners. One approach is simply to work with students with white boards in a semi-circle. Present a problem and go to work. On the count of three, display your boards, including the teacher's work. A math teacher I observed years ago had a most effective feedback tool. On their math worksheets, he strategically situated stop signs every few problems. Students knew to stop, work that problem on a sticky note, and place it on the board. The teacher met them at the board, and they collaborated on the work. It provided this private tutorial session just when needed. The teacher then told them they were ready to move to the next set of problems.

- **Weave in peer tutoring.** Each partner or group member works alone first. Now, they share answers and discuss how they arrived at their answers. Is there a consensus?
- **Provide answer keys or model work as needed.** This is especially valuable during stations, in which teachers simply cannot be everywhere to provide feedback. In addition, a quick video in which teachers provide answers or explanations can move learning forward.
- **Connect academic success to controllable factors.** Successful learners tend to believe that their progress is attributable to hard work. Students who are struggling academically often believe something quite different—that they are incapable of learning the concepts (Mendler, 2000). While educators implore them to work harder, their thought pattern might just be, "Why work any harder? I am never going to get this." Therefore, feedback to students should include commendations for hard work and tenacity.
- **Be as authentically hopeful as possible.** Providing feedback to an academically fragile—and perhaps defensive—student takes finesse. There might be a sea of errors in their writing—is there an area of originality in their thinking that can be genuinely commended before we tactically approach the lack of structure?
- **What about students who are not even getting started?** Recently, I observed a teacher with a marvelous approach. She simply stopped by the student's desk and asked, "Are you having trouble getting started today? Sometimes that happens with me. Here's what I do…" My approach has always been to set a small goal with students in that situation. "I'm going to visit with some other students for a bit. While I'm gone, what do you think would be a reasonable goal? I let them tell me. "Super, I'll check on you in a few minutes. I feel confident that you can meet that goal."

Goal-setting and ongoing, descriptive feedback to reach those goals are known motivators. Their work is our feedback for the progress they are making. Therefore, work must be as visible as possible. The student-centered classroom enables multiple opportunities to monitor their progress and provide concrete steps for improvement.

## START WITH SUCCESS

Success is addictive. It feels good to solve a problem, to share a good idea, or have a lab experiment go well. Acknowledgement by a teacher or team member fuels us. Even flipping over an answer key on our own and seeing that our response is a match encourages us to continue to work. There is a reason that many of the same students raise their hands day after day, year after year. Their academic histories indicate that the answer they want to share is close to correct and that a commendation will immediately come their way. Hands pop up. It is a safe bet. Other students work hard to stay off the radar and avoid answering questions. And so it continues—a handful of students move lessons forward while others avoid participating and any potential risk of embarrassment that may follow.

Changing this pattern—moving ALL students to active engagement- starts with the opening minutes. Leaders often ask me where the journey to increased academic achievement begins—where to start. My answer: The opening minutes. When I work with new teachers the answer is the same—refine the opening minutes of learning. Why? The opening minutes have the power to create genuine success in ALL learners, to tap into their strengths, to hear their ideas, to imbed prior knowledge, and to even have a little fun. Bland warm-ups and searching for homework are quite possibly the last thing learners' brains need in the opening minutes.

Motivation and success begin in the opening minutes. Is there value and relevance in what we are about to learn? Yes! What about confidence, the second critical piece for active engagement? With well-constructed openers—Yes! But even if it is a maybe, the value of the task can propel participation simply because the task is so captivating. Plus, their work during the opening minutes provides visible evidence for feedback and encouragement. And their brains are getting that pop that more successful students get—they are off to a good start in class!

Furthermore, success starters that captivate, engage, and imbed prior knowledge spark intellectual curiosity. A desire to learn more about a concept begins in the opening minutes. Success starters should prepare brains for listening to the mini lesson. Students' brains tire. The opener can help extend engagement into the lesson portion.

Effective success starters typically contain these elements:

- High interest
- Intellectual curiosity
- Prior knowledge development
- Clear connection to learning target
- Motivation to hear and learn more
- 100% engagement

In other words, success starters are often the most intriguing part of a learning experience. These short tasks, often done with a partner or team, spark an interest in hearing more about the concept. These might include demonstrations, thought-provoking questions, current events/sports, hands-on learning, brainstorming, visuals, or games.

What do success starters sound and look like? Below are some examples:

Students: Something crazy is going in baseball! Last night, an MLB batter came up to bat and took a big swing. The ball came off the bat at 103 MPH and the trajectory was on target for a homerun. The announcers shrieked, "That's out of here!" And then the ball plopped into the center fielder's glove for an easy out. Here's the mystery that you and your partner will be solving: Where have all the homeruns gone this season? What is different? And yes, you can use your phones. Put your ideas on a sticky note and post them on the board. Students will discover that small changes to the stitches have changed the game. What they will be learning in physics: drag.

Students: You are about to see eight slides. With a partner or team, create a simple T chart on a sticky note with two headings: Interest Rates and Home Prices. First, you will simply record the data from the past four months for each category. Next, you will look for patterns and relationships. On your own, teams will determine the relationship between interest rates and home prices. Next, explain your reasoning. You have four minutes...

Students: We are about to read *The Great Gatsby*. Fitzgerald uses the setting of the novel to establish themes. With your partner, look at the following slides that depict The Jazz Age and the northern shores of Long Island, New York. Look for clues as to the year, the economy, and culture. Describe your initial impression using just five words.

Students: Before we embark on our unit on civilizations, you will be working in teams to demonstrate what you already know. On your tables are sorts. First, your team will organize the slips that belong together. Next, create 5-6 categories. For example, fashion, food, sports, and language might belong together. You may decide that these all fit under the category of culture. At the end of this exercise, you will answer this question, "What are the five traits of a civilization?"

Students: Look at the picture of this cargo ship loaded with 500 containers. It was stuck in the mud for an entire month. Some very bright people tried different approaches to no avail. In your teams, your job is to dislodge the ship. Using everything you have learned in math and science thus far, how would your team solve this problem? (They finally got it on the third try!) Students will soon learn just how smart they are—the team that solved the problem waited for a full moon!

Link: https://www.foxbusiness.com/economy/ever-forward-container-ship-stuck-chesapeake-bay-month-finally-freed

Students: We are going to be talking about a critical historical invention today, the cotton gin. But first, in teams, you will determine the impact of a familiar invention—the cell phone. How has the cell phone impacted the economy, the environment, and the social fabric of the world? Your four minutes begins now. After this opener, students learn about the cotton gin. At the end of the lesson, students make their case: Which invention had the bigger impact on the world—the cotton gin or the cell phone? The relevant cell phone opener sets up the cotton gin—the big technology of an earlier time.

Students: We are going to be learning about snails today. Everyone in here has some knowledge of snails, right? Let's kick this off in partners with an AGREE/DISAGREE. What are your thoughts?

Note: Agree/Disagree in math may have statements like "The x-axis and y-axis run parallel to each other." In ELA, "There is no need to cite an author if you had the same idea, too."

Students: We have been learning about how to calculate the percent of increase. To continue our work, you and your partner will be figuring out where the mathematical error lies in someone else's work. First, find the error in the following business article. Then, explain the correct approach to the problem. Finally, why does this matter?

"Small business owners are having trouble paying their rent. The business magazine, "Biz Today" details that in November, 37% of small business owners surveyed reported that they were unable to pay their rent. The rate of delinquency was 30% in October. The 7% increase represented the largest increase month to month all year."

| AGREE/DISAGREE | The trail of mucus snails leave helps them find their way home. |
|---|---|
| AGREE/DISAGREE | Snails hibernate in the winter. |
| AGREE/DISAGREE | Snail racing is an organized sport. |
| AGREE/DISAGREE | Snails are mollusks and lack internal skeletons and bones. |
| AGREE/DISAGREE | Snails fee exclusively on plants. |
| AGREE/DISAGREE | The shell on snails grows. |
| AGREE/DISAGREE | Most snails have both male and female reproductive parts. |
| AGREE/DISAGREE | Snails live all over the world. |

This is an example of an error analysis, a higher-level thinking strategy that requires prior knowledge. Students enjoy these, but they are best incorporated deep into units. And while some consider error analysis to belong to the math domain, these fit nicely across disciplines. Branches of government, types of economics, electrical currents, cells—this strategy provides an opportunity for all learners to stretch.

The examples above demonstrate the difference between what I term "Success Starters" with traditional warm-ups. With this approach, innovation, thinking, and excitement go first. This is in direct contrast to the largely classroom management practice of getting something for students to do in the opening minutes so that administrative tasks can be handled—to get kids out of the halls and in desks.

Success is addictive. These strategies are directly connected to the targets, but often on a higher plane of thinking. They are frequently collaborative, relevant, and rarely graded. They tap into (or develop) prior knowledge and spark intellectual curiosity. And they motivate. Be it a core or acceleration class—we always start with something captivating. These strategies enable learners to start off with genuine success, collaborate with a peer, and receive feedback. And after they start off strong, it is much easier to build upon that success.

---

## YOUR TURN:

Compare & contrast success starters with warm-ups by purpose, traits, and examples.

---

The strategies detailed here boost intrinsic motivation. Intrinsic motivation is genuine. Without rewards being dangled or punishments looming, they actually want to do this work. Here is a list of what was detailed above:

To increase student motivation, instill or increase these practices:

- Student autonomy
- Vicarious learning experiences
- The value of tasks
- Goal setting
- Ongoing feedback
- Success in the opening minutes

What is missing from the list? Extrinsic motivators. While these may support some students in behavioral goals, extrinsic motivators can actually harm students. They can negatively influence performance on subsequent tasks and can reduce tenacity and interest on more challenging tasks. When rewards were given for simply completing a task, students' intrinsic motivation actually declines. (Deci, Koestner, and Ryan, 2001). Sadly, the one area in which rewards work: when the tasks were so dull no one wanted to do them anyway... In sum, rewards for completing academic tasks should be used sparingly. Success and genuine accomplishment build self-efficacy, not prizes.

Extracurricular activities may not fall completely under motivation, but research has shown that students who engage in these do better in school. One thought is that students forge connections with faculty members about areas of common interest. The conversations with teachers are not all about math, science, or make-up work. In addition, students demonstrate strengths they may lack in the academic realm. School is a more positive place for students who engage in extracurricular activities. Chess clubs, drums, art, drama, sports—extracurricular activities support students in important ways.

For academically challenged learners, motivation is often a lingering issue. They have fallen out of the success loop. They understandably may not participate as readily; in fact, they may not even sign up for tutoring or other programs. They still crave success—it just hasn't happened in a while. Acceleration in itself is motivational—they are provided just enough of a sneak peek to know some answers in advance of class. Below is a table of instructional practices that can motivate even the most reluctant learners. Personalize the following list of motivating practices with ideas for your students.

## SUMMARY

Motivational strategies for students who are behind might look different than what we had thought. The way lessons are crafted and implemented impact motivation. Prizes may add some fun to school, but they do not build intrinsic motivation. The self-efficacy of the teacher in the classroom and the students surrounding those who are struggling increase motivation. Clear goals, dynamic openers, student autonomy, and ongoing feedback move learning. The value of the tasks is paramount. Learners need a strong reason to jump in and try again. Relevant, exciting tasks can circumvent messages about past failures.

But while there is a connection between the learning experiences and student motivation, this does not mean that children will not demonstrate off-task behaviors, get frustrated, or simply have bad days. Even the most enthralling, motivational lessons will not remedy everything. What they will do, however, is create small successes that spark more effort and more engagement. These strategies work together during learning to nudge all students back into the success loop, where hands go up. Because success on a task feels pretty great.

## YOUR TURN:

Six ways to boost motivation are below. In the spaces, translate these ideas into tangible classroom strategies.

| | |
|---|---|
| Goal Setting | |
| Opening Minutes | |
| Value of Tasks | |
| Vicarious Experiences | |
| Ongoing Feedback | |
| Student Autonomy | |

## YOUR TURN:

What steps can be taken to increase student motivation?

What is the appropriate balance between intrinsic and extrinsic motivators?

On a scale of 1-10, how motivated are your learners? Why?

# 6
## PRINCIPLES OF ACCELERATION

A S PRESENTED THROUGHOUT this workbook, there are overarching principles of acceleration. The principles listed below are a starting point. At the end of the five principles is an exercise with three categories: Practices to Increase, Practices to Decrease, and Practices to Eliminate. After reading the principles below, respond with ideas from your school. Next, consider this: are there additional principles that should be added?

## PRINCIPLE ONE

The process of acceleration relies on a cohesive connection between core and acceleration teachers. These two instructional entities move together collaboratively with a common purpose of academic success on today and tomorrow's learning targets. Traditional remediation programs are often constructed from a list of deficits, often determined by a preassessment. Any bearing on today's learning is largely coincidental. Acceleration, conversely, is purposeful, anticipatory, and laser-focused on new learning targets. Learning experiences in acceleration are tailored to bring success in the core class. Ongoing communication between educators in both components is paramount. Acceleration prepares students for new learning but also provides extra practice or reteaching based on ongoing feedback from their core teacher. Acceleration is largely formative and contributes to mastery, but the core class is the mastery experience.

What gauges are utilized to determine how acceleration is working? Ongoing student work, student engagement, and soft assessments, such as white boards, and problems answered right on their desks, provide data on what is working during acceleration. However, the most important indicator of success is how students are doing in their core class. Are their grades going up? Are acceleration students contributing more? Are they working harder? Are they more confident? When in doubt, ask them. For example:

- Tell me what worked on this lesson and next steps that would be helpful.
- What changes in the lesson would have made you more successful?
- Give a review of that lesson from 1-5 stars and leave a comment.
- On this chart paper, there are three categories. Stick your dots on what would most build success: More Practice, More Relevance, More Work in Teams

Acceleration is a very intentional, tightly woven collaborative process. Traditional remediation is often parallel in nature; consequently, content intersections are often coincidental. In acceleration, these two instructional worlds merge purposefully—students are provided exactly what they need to learn new targets today, right alongside their peers. Because the last thing these learners need is to acquire additional gaps.

Acceleration strategies are impactful and engaging, but these techniques also work well in the core class. Scaffolding, captivating openers, student autonomy, quick feedback, visible learning, high interest and relevance: these move students upwards and should be employed in every classroom.

## PRINCIPLE TWO

Acceleration is forward moving. Instruction is just ahead of core instruction while also addressing critical past gaps needed for today. Acceleration contains three components. Teachers will:

1. Imbed prior knowledge development that will speed up processing of new information during the mastery experience. If students are poised to learn about planets in their core class, acceleration students might watch a video on planets or read a picture book about planets. For vocabulary, students may head outside to practice being in an orbit and learn the words elliptical and rotate. In this example, prior knowledge includes experiences, background knowledge, and vocabulary.

2. Create or provide scaffolding devices that move forward with students. In math, these might include multiplication bookmarks. In language arts, a cheat sheet on transition words or figurative language might be scaffolded. These references go with students to their core class.

3. Provide remediation as needed just in time (JIT) for new learning. This may look like one station or small group with practice on a past skill that will be required today. If all students need additional support, this might also be in a whole group setting. In addition, extra practice on new skills may be folded into acceleration. This ad hoc remediation is based on ongoing collaboration with the core partner.

In all three components above, the instructional focus is on success today. There are standards in which no remediation or scaffolding is required. Others have quite a bit. The 80-20 recommendation is a gauge to avoid the gravitation pull to pick up every piece students have missed. Older students, by simply being exposed to so much content, often have a substantial list of gaps. Backwards movement can be a futile path for learners. In addition, learning is simply easier when it is in context and applied today.

## PRINCIPLE THREE

Acceleration is perhaps as much of a shift in mindset as it is a change in instruction. Some of these students enter the classroom with an expectation of failure. They may not think they are able to be successful in the subject. Defeatism, rather than optimism, may be their mindset. Their self-efficacy may be understandably low. But self-efficacy is not fixed; rather, it is quite malleable. Confidence can be rebuilt, one poem, one planet, or one math problem at a time.

High expectations of learners—seeing them as potential success stories—is critical. An excitement for the content, the thrill of learners getting the hang of something. A fresh start matters. Teachers who see student's futures rather than their pasts might look like a welcome at the door, or a congratulatory note on a success. It might be an acknowledgement that today we will get better as we work through some content issues...together. Instructional optimism in the face of pessimism is important but it must be genuine. They know they are behind. The message is, "This is doable. You've got this."

Academically vulnerable learners, especially older ones, often arrive with common traits. Low self-efficacy, frustration, and a fear of continued failure may have accompanied them into the room today. A demeanor of feigned disinterest may be presented. They have probably been grouped for this class; therefore, some teachers (understandably) might be reluctant to venture into more engaging practices out of behavioral concerns...or a remedial mindset. Acceleration is strength-based to restart success and rebuild habits. In sum, successful acceleration experiences are tailor made for unique traits that many vulnerable learners possess.

## PRINCIPLE FOUR

"This Doesn't Look Like a Support Class." That is what observers should say when visiting acceleration classes. High-impact practices, relevance, hands-on learning, collaborations, adventures—anything but a worksheet. Why? Because to move students quickly who are behind depends on high impact, captivating instruction.

Many teachers rely on stations to immerse students on the target and to boost engagement. One station might utilize courseware, but lessons there should serve to meet the current target. A second lesson might be tactile, with sorts, cubes, or manipulatives. The third might be teacher modeling and student whiteboards. Error analysis, sticky note problems, agree/disagrees, games—the possibilities are endless for stations.

Be it stations or games or determining the perimeter of the football field—the common thread is this: instruction is enthralling, not tedious. To overcome motivational issues requires a lively, fast-paced, often hands-on classroom. To boost academic success in students who are behind requires the best practices teachers can muster. Open with something captivating, provide descriptive feedback and genuine encouragement, create student-centered lessons with opportunities for autonomy, and incorporate tasks for small successes upon which to build.

## PRINCIPLE FIVE

Acceleration supports student motivation, particularly for those who are in the throes of academic failure. Motivation to initiate work on a task comes from within. Motivation to sustain effort when frustration sets in also comes from within. But lesson components, teacher support, and classroom environment all help to boost motivation.

Compelling, nongraded openers and clear goals increase motivation. Student-centered learning with opportunities for choice and autonomy make students want to jump in. Small tasks, fewer problems, and shorter pieces of text often yield better results. A mystery envelope on the table with two fractions to place on a number line will spur their imaginations more than something on a tablet. Those opportunities provide avenues for quick, ongoing, growth-oriented feedback, an essential element to moving learning upward quickly. Feedback begins with seeing their work—from the opening minutes to the middle of the lesson to the closing minutes.

Students who have lacked success in school for a while may be understandably reluctant to share their work. Arms over papers, screens half-way down, or withdrawal from tasks completely. But work doesn't have to look like work at all. Sorts also serve as formative assessments, as do writing on desks or chart paper. Games—both digital and "old school" yield data. Through a growth lens, everything students create during acceleration provide insights into their progress. Rather than put papers in bins or store in digital files, provide immediate feedback now. Commend growth and hard work.

Vicarious experiences, a known motivator, depend first on the teacher's enthusiasm and self-efficacy. Why? Learners soak up some of the teacher's confidence. In the acceleration classroom, students who are struggling are likely sitting next to other students in the same academic situation. Therefore, students may not get that upward motivational pull of a confident neighbor enjoying their work. As they improve, their confidence should rise, which will positively impact adjacent learners.

In the table below, consider practices that align with acceleration principles. For example, worksheets might be an item to decrease. Courseware might be listed as an area for more tactical use. Communication between the core and acceleration classes might warrant an increase. Summative assessments might be an area to eliminate during acceleration.

## FINAL THOUGHTS

Imagine being terrible at one's job. A sense of dread creeps in on the drive to work. The boss hovers nearby, ready to pounce on errors, missing reports, or for simply arriving five minutes late. Worry escalates about an upcoming employee evaluation or even a potential termination. Avoidance by colleagues and lack of praise by supervisors adds to the stress. Others at work get better assignments and are called on for ideas at meetings. Avoidance—staying off the radar—becomes a critical strategy. If things do not improve, however, there is a way out—to pursue a different position elsewhere.

Students do not have the options adults have or the years of experience in managing challenging situations. The bus arrives at the same place every day. One can make the case that—perhaps despite their nonchalant or callous exteriors—these learners feel terrible about their current academic situations.

Acceleration is a strength-based approach that enables students to start again—to find success at school once more...even if it has been a while. By setting up success on today's target, they can rejoin the academic fold—to move away from the back of the room into the center of classroom experiences. Acceleration is ambitious and encouraging, but it also pragmatic and research driven. The promise of acceleration is that we will never give up on our learners who have fallen behind. Acceleration is an imperfect process that requires ongoing adjustments, collaboration, and thoughtful planning. But seeing hands up again make the effort so worthwhile.

# YOUR TURN:

Practices to Increase, Decrease, Or Eliminate

| Principle | Increase | Decrease | Eliminate |
|---|---|---|---|
| Connection Between Core/ Acceleration | | | |
| Forward Moving with JIT Remediation | | | |
| Mindset & Expectations | | | |
| Captivating Instruction | | | |
| Intrinsic Motivation | | | |

# REFERENCES

Adult Literacy Facts. (2019). Retrieved from https://proliteracy.org

Anderson, G., Whipple, A., & Jimerson, S. (2003). Grade retention: Achievement and mental health outcomes. Center for Development and Learning.

Brophy, J. (2010). Motivating students to learn. New York: Routeledge.

Davies, A. (2007). Involving students in the classroom assessment process. In D. Reeves *Ahead of the curve: The power of assessment to transform teaching and learning,* 31-57.

Deci, E.L., Koestner, R, & Ryan, R.M. (2001). Extrinsic rewards and intrinsic motivation in education: Reconsidered once again. *Review of Educational Research,* 71(1), 1-27.

Eccles, J.S.et al. (1993). Negative effects of traditional middle schools on students' motivation. The Elementary School Journal. 93(5), 553-574.

Galuschka, K., & Schulte-Korne, G. (2016). The diagnosis and treatment of reading and/or spelling disorders in children and adolescents. *Deutsches Arzteblatt International,* 113(6), 279-286.

Hansen, D. (1989). Lesson evading and lesson dissembling: Ego strategies in the classroom. *American Journal of Education,* 97(2), 184-208.

Harlen, W. & Crick, R. (2003). Testing and motivation for learning. Assessment in Education, 10(2), 169-207.

Hattie, J. & Yates, G. (2014). *Visible learning and the science of how we learn.* New York: Routeledge.

Hoy, A. & Davis, H. (2006). Teacher self-efficacy and its influence on the achievement of adolescents. In F. Pajares & T. Urdan (eds.), *Self-efficacy beliefs of adolescents* (pp. 71-96), Greenwich, CT: Information Age Publishing.

Jimerson, S., Anderson, G., & Whipple, A. (2002) Winning the battle and losing the war: Examining the relation between grade retention and dropping out of high school. *Psychology in the Schools.* 39(4), 441-457.

Kanno, Y., & Cromley, J. (2015). English language learners' pathways to four-year colleges. *Teachers College Record,* 117(120306).

Marzano, R.I. (2004). *Building Background Knowledge for Academic Achievement: Research on what works in schools.* Alexandria, VA (ASCD).

Morgan, P.L., Farkas, G., & Wu, Q. (2012) Do poor readers fees angry, sad, unpopular? *Scientific Studies of Reading,* 16(4), 360-381.

Murphey, D. (2014). The academic achievement of English language learners. *Child Trends,* 2014-62.

Rollins, SP. (2020). Teaching vulnerable learners. New York, NY. W.W. Norton

Schunk, D.H. & Meese, J.L. (2006). Self-efficacy development in adolescence. In F. Pajares & T. Urdan (eds.), *Self-efficacy beliefs of adolescents* (pp. 71-96), Greenwich, CT: Information Age Publishing.

Silberflitt,B., Jimerson, S., Burns, M., & Appleton, J. (2006). Does the timing of grade retention make a difference? Examining the effects of early versus later retention. *School Psychology Review.* 35(1), 134-141.

Stanovich, K.E. (1986). Matthew effects in reading: Some consequences of individual differences in the acquisition of literacy. Reading Research Quarterly, 21(4). 360-406.

Usher, E. & Pajares, F. (2008). Sources of self-efficacy in school: Critical review of the literature and future directions. *Review of Educational Research,* 78(4), 751-796.

Van de Pol, I, Volman, M. & Beishuizen, I. (2010). Scaffolding in teacher-student interaction: A decade of research. *Educational Psychology Review,* 22(3), 271-196.

Willis, J. (2006). *Research-based strategies to ignite student learning.* Alexandria, VA. ASCD.

Yair, G. (2000). Educational battlefields in America: The tug-of-war over students' engagement with instruction. *Sociology of Education,* 73(4). 247-269.

# ABOUT THE AUTHOR

Suzy Pepper Rollins is an author, consultant, and speaker who works with schools across North America to create success in ALL learners. Her particular passion is to change the academic trajectory of vulnerable learners. She is the author of *Learning in the Fast Lane* and *Teaching in the Fast Lane*, both by ASCD. Her book *Teaching Vulnerable Learners* (W.W. Norton) details strategies for students who are bored, discouraged, or just ready to give up.

In addition, she is the founder of Math in the Fast Lane, which aligns with her principles of captivating, hands-on tasks. (www.MathinFastLane.com.) Suzy can be reached at her website, www.SuzyPepperRollins.com or via Twitter @myedexpert.

Made in United States
North Haven, CT
09 June 2023

37515343R00041